WATERLOO
1815

Waterloo 1815

Wavre, Plancenoit and the Race to Paris

Peter Hofschröer

Pen & Sword
MILITARY

First published in Great Britain in 2006 by
Pen & Sword Military
an imprint of
Pen & Sword Books Ltd
47 Church Street
Barnsley
South Yorkshire
S70 2AS

ISBN 1-84415-176-X

A CIP catalogue record for this book is available from the British
Library

Typeset in 10pt Palatino by
Mac Style, Nafferton, E. Yorkshire

Printed and bound in the UK by
CPI

Pen & Sword Books Ltd incorporates the Imprints of Pen & Sword
Aviation, Pen & Sword Maritime, Pen & Sword Military, Wharncliffe
Local History, Pen and Sword Select, Pen and Sword Military Classics
and Leo Cooper.

For a complete list of Pen & Sword titles please contact
PEN & SWORD BOOKS LIMITED
47 Church Street, Barnsley, South Yorkshire, S70 2AS, England
E-mail: enquiries@pen-and-sword.co.uk
Website: www.pen-and-sword.co.uk

CONTENTS

Acknowledgements 6

Introduction 7

1 The Retreat to Wavre 9

2 The Night in Wavre 19

3 The Strategic Position 27

4 The March to Plancenoit 32

5 Plancenoit 43

6 The Battle of Wavre, 18/19 June 1815 64

7 The Aftermath 74

8 The Four Armies 101

9 Tour Guide 110

Orders of battle 125

Recommended further reading 129

Index 131

ACKNOWLEDGEMENTS

My thanks go to Hasso Count Bülow von Dennewitz and Major (ret.) Graeme Cooper, both of whom have accompanied me on my tours to the Waterloo area.

INTRODUCTION

Histories of the Waterloo Campaign generally concentrate on the main battle, leaving the role of the Prussian and Federal German armies in the background. Little has been said of what was surely Lt-General Count Neidhardt von Gneisenau's greatest contribution to the final downfall of Napoleon – the way in which he rallied the defeated Prussians, turning chaos into order and transforming a tactical defeat into a strategic victory. Left with the bitter taste of defeat in their mouths, and for a time without leadership, these men conducted an exhausting overnight march to Wavre, where they had only the briefest of respites, before being sent on to make the decisive attack at the Battle of Waterloo. This achievement was all the more remarkable as much of the Prussian infantry was militia and faced its baptism of fire on 16 June 1815. Furthermore, Lt-General Hans von Zieten's Corps had suffered nearly 40 percent losses in the first two days of the fighting, yet, on the morning of 18 June, it took the bit between its teeth again and made its march to Waterloo, allowing the Duke of Wellington's battered centre to be relieved just in time to receive Napoleon's final thrust, the attack of the Imperial Guard.

The route Field Marshal Prince Blücher von Wahlstadt's army took to Waterloo on 18 June 1815 was twisted and tortuous. His army was exhausted and disorganised *before* it even started its march to Waterloo. A fire in the narrow streets of Wavre delayed it, then the torrential rain of the previous night turned the narrow paths to Plancenoit into mudslides, along which moving the artillery and waggons proved difficult. Only by walking the route can the superhuman efforts Blücher made to keep his word to Wellington be fully appreciated.

If that was not enough, Blücher's exhausted and ravenous men, covered from head to foot in mud and dirt and suffering from a raging thirst, faced Napoleon Bonaparte's élite Imperial Guard, rested and fed, waiting for them in the village stronghold of Plancenoit, with its fortress-like church. The battle began for the right rear of Napoleon's position, the key to victory. Facing such determined opposition, the Prussians had to storm the village three times before they finally imposed their will. With the road in the rear of Napoleon's position now open to them, the Battle of Waterloo was won. Indeed, as Sir Richard Hussey Vivian, commander of a cavalry brigade in Wellington's army, put it:

> ... Too little [is] allowed for the support and assistance of the Prussians on this great occasion. That the British and their allies fought most determinately, and held their position with a degree of obstinacy and courage with which Napoleon had never been before resisted, it must be admitted; but when it is considered how large a Prussian force came to their assistance, attacking the right flank and, rear of the French, no military man can refuse to attribute to such assistance a considerable share in the brilliant victory that followed without such assistance the British might have held their ground, but the defeat of the enemy never could have been so complete.

Determined to bring the weight of numbers to bear at the crucial point at Waterloo, the Prussian high command left Lt-General Johann Adolf von Thielemann's III Army Corps behind at Wavre to cover their rear and to suffer its fate at the hands of Marshal Emmanuel de Grouchy's pursuing Frenchmen. Thielemann's men held on, and only just, against overwhelming odds, until the news of victory at Waterloo arrived.

The Prussians then went over to the offensive and the pursuit to Paris started. Grouchy, now able to act on his own initiative, withdrew and, once no longer acting on Napoleon's orders, came into his own, conducting a brilliant rearguard action. Grouchy's actions kept alive the possibility for Napoleon to rally his defeated forces and continue the campaign.

History often regards the Waterloo Campaign as having ended with the battle of that name, but there was every chance Napoleon might have bounced back after that defeat, as he had done so often in the past, and rallied his troops on Grouchy's wing and used the northern French fortresses as a base of operations. Blücher's vigorous pursuit to Paris did much to prevent that happening, but pro-Bonapartist fortresses held out for months after Napoleon had surrendered to the British, the last one capitulating on 30 November 1815, marking the end of the Waterloo Campaign.

Chapter One

The Retreat to Wavre

Positions of the three armies

On the evening of 16 June 1815, Napoleon's main army, consisting of the Imperial Guard, the infantry corps of General Dominique-Joseph-René Vandamme, Count d'Unsebourg; Marshal Maurice-Étienne Count Gérard and Marshal Georges Mouton Count de Lobau; the infantry division of General Baron Jean-Baptiste Girard from the corps of Marshal Honoré-Charles-Michel-Joseph Count Reille and the cavalry corps of General Claude-Pierre Count Pajol; General Rémy-Joseph-Isodore Baron Exelmans and General Edouard-Jean-Baptiste Count Milhaud under the command of Marshal Emmanuel Count de Grouchy, was situated on the field of Ligny, which had just been taken from the Prussians.

The wing of the army under the command of Marshal Michel Ney, Count of Moscow, consisting of the infantry corps of Reille and the cavalry corps of General Count François-Étienne Kellermann, Duke of Valmy, was facing the forces under the Duke of Wellington in and around Quatre Bras. The infantry corps under Marshal Jean-Baptiste Drouet Count d'Erlon was between Quatre Bras and Ligny, not having been involved in either battle that day. The main part of the Duke of Wellington's army was either at Quatre Bras or on its way there, but would withdraw to Waterloo the next morning.

The French Imperial Guard infantry. It was in the bitter fighting for possession of the village of Plancenoit that Napoleon's much vaunted Guard scored its last success. It was to suffer its final defeat only an hour or so later.

French Imperial Guard Chasseur. Consisting of infantry, cavalry and artillery, the Imperial Guard made up one corps in Napoleon's army. The Guard Cavalry was frittered away on 18 June 1815 attacking Wellington's squares.

The Prussian army, under the nominal command of Field Marshal Prince Blücher von Wahlstadt, consisted of four army corps of mixed arms. The first two, under Lt-General Hans von Zieten and Major-General Georg Dubislav Ludwig von Pirch I, were falling back from Ligny in the general direction of Wavre. The third, under Lt-General Johann Adolf von Thielemann, was falling back from Ligny towards Gembloux. The fourth, under General Friedrich Wilhelm Count Bülow von Dennewitz, was coming up from Namur to Gembloux.

The situation after the Battle of Ligny

On 16 June, Napoleon's final attack on the Prussian centre at Ligny, made in the growing darkness, achieved the long-awaited breakthrough. Blücher tried to stem this last assault at the head of his cavalry, but fell beneath his mortally injured mount leading an unsuccessful charge. With the commander-in-chief *hors de combat* and confused masses of men falling back, control was lost for a time. The Prussian right wing fell back to the north, as did the centre. The left wing headed east, towards Gembloux, where reinforcements in the shape of Bülow's IV Army Corps were expected. No decision had been made before the battle on a line of retreat; any withdrawal was to be made according to circumstances and that was impossible to predict.

History often presents Gneisenau, the Prussian chief-of-staff, as having an irrational mistrust of his ally Wellington, and wanting to take his beaten army eastwards, towards home. Such tales originate from Lt-Colonel Sir Henry Hardinge, Wellington's liaison officer in Blücher's headquarters, but he was known for telling several tall stories about this affair. Furthermore, an examination of the record – both documentary and eyewitness – shows this not to be true. Gneisenau's first action was to ensure that no further men took to the road east towards Namur, but he was not able to stop around 8,000 men from departing for the Rhineland. He then attempted to direct the remainder of the army on the village of Tilly, just a few kilometres north of Brye, the last village his men had held on that day's battlefield. From Tilly, there were roads running westwards, along which Gneisenau could have taken his army to just behind Wellington's position at Quatre Bras. This act makes his intention clear.

Sir Henry Hardinge. In the Waterloo Campaign, Hardinge was Wellington's representative in the Prussian headquarters. His reported accounts of certain incidents have given rise to a number of myths.

This was, however, not to be, but that was not due to any decisions Gneisenau made. The Prussian forces had spent much of that day involved in street fighting, a form of battle which easily breaks down the cohesion of units and in which command and control are quickly lost. Added to that were the heavy casualties that particularly Zieten (39%) and Pirch I (17%) had suffered, further destroying the integrity of these units. Finally, many of these men were untried and poorly trained militia fighting their first battle. Lacking much in the way of military experience, one cannot reasonably expect them to maintain their order for long. Gneisenau was simply not able to stop this disordered mass of men where he wanted to. It continued through Tilly and beyond.

Having done what he could to regain control over his shattered army, Gneisenau then looked for a suitable place to establish his headquarters. A report came to him that Blücher had been located and was recovering in Mellery, a few kilometres north of Tilly. Moving through Mellery, he found a group of soldiers guarding a house at the far end of the village. Gneisenau had found his master. Order was slowly being restored.

Now that the headquarters had come together again, orders could be despatched to the army. A staff officer was sent off with orders for the retreating column. He rode for many kilometres, down dark and narrow country lanes, before reaching the head of the column at Lauzelle, just south of Wavre. In effect, the army had chosen its line of retreat, the men voting with their feet. At this time, the road ran

NAPOLEON BONAPARTE (1769–1821)

The man that shaped this era was born in Ajaccio, on the isle of Corsica. He spent his youth training to be an artilleryman in the French army, in the country that had recently annexed the Italian-speaking island, until then part of the Republic of Genoa. His early career was nondescript, but in 1793 his handling of the artillery that broke the siege of the British-occupied French Mediterranean port of Toulon catapulted him into the limelight. His experience in the Italian Campaign of 1794 stood him in good stead and the 'whiff of grapeshot' with which he broke the power of the Paris mob in 1795 opened the door for a career in politics. His successful campaign in Italy in 1796 laid the foundations of his power-base in the army. Despite suffering a setback in his Egyptian adventure, Napoleon seized power in 1799 after his return to France as one of three consuls that swept away the corrupt and unpopular Directory. He was soon made into First Consul and became the supreme ruler of France.

Napoleon's second campaign in Italy in 1800 did much to consolidate his power in France, and in 1804 he crowned himself emperor. At this time, France was, after Russia, the second most populous state in Europe. Its colonial possessions and international trading network rivalled that of Britain. Napoleon massed a large army at Boulogne on the Channel and made it look as if he were going to invade Britain. Instead, Napoleon took this well-trained force into Central Europe in 1805, defeating the Austrians at Ulm and then a joint Austro-Russian force at Austerlitz. His crowning success came in the campaign of 1806 at Jena and Auerstedt against Prussia, in which he destroyed the military capabilities of this great power in a matter of days. He consolidated his hold on Central Europe with the Peace of Tilsit, made with Russia in 1807.

Next, Napoleon turned his attention to the Iberian peninsula, where he tried to install his brother Joseph as king. The popular uprising against foreign occupation turned into the 'Spanish Ulcer' and the war in the peninsula that was to wear down France's military power. It also gave Arthur Wellesley, later the Duke of Wellington, the platform from which he launched his rise to fame and power. Wellington would achieve in Spain and Portugal what Nelson had accomplished at the Battle of Trafalgar in 1805.

The first serious attempt to shake off Napoleon's hold on Central Europe came in 1809, with the War of the Fifth Coalition. Despite a setback at Aspern-Essling near Vienna at the hands of the Austrian Archduke Charles,

Napoleon's will eventually prevailed with his victory at Wagram just weeks later. He remained master of Central Europe.

The Continental System, Napoleon's blockade in reverse, led to a conflict with Russia. He assembled the greatest army yet seen and invaded Russia in 1812. He reached Moscow, but the vastness of the country swallowed up so much of his force that, unable to supply his army, he turned for home. Marshal Winter and the Cossacks dealt with most of what remained of this once proud army. There was now a power vacuum in Central Europe.

A popular uprising in East Prussia precipitated what became known as the Wars of Liberation. First Prussia joined the Czar in the spring of 1813, followed by Austria in the summer. Britain doled out guineas and gunpowder to all that agreed to fight against Napoleon. For a while, Napoleon showed signs of regaining his hold over Central Europe, but weight of numbers eventually prevailed, and his defeat at the Battle of Nations in Leipzig that October sealed his fate. France fell in 1814, and Napoleon was sent into exile on the Mediterranean island of Elba.

Escaping from captivity, Napoleon landed in the south of France at the beginning of March 1815, precipitating a series of events known as the 'Hundred Days', in which the Battle of Waterloo was the most dramatic event. After this defeat, Napoleon returned to Paris, but lacking support, he surrendered to the British and was sent to the isolated island of St Helena in the southern Atlantic, where he saw out his remaining days.

Napoleon was one of the great captains of history and many feared him. At this time, his record on the field of battle was second-to-none.

through a wood, and just three officers blocked it. The army was halted. Dawn was breaking.

En route, many officers had sought to rally their units, calling their men together. As it fell back, this defeated mass of Prussians was slowly being transformed into an army again. A disorderly retreat was becoming an orderly withdrawal. The withdrawal would turn into an advance. The advance would achieve victory.

A report on the situation at the head of the army was sent back to headquarters. The order came up the line to continue this movement just a little further. Zieten was ordered to bivouac at Bierges, a little to the south-west of Wavre, and on the far side of the Dyle River. Pirch I was told to take his men to Ste-Anne, to the north of the town. Thielemann was sent on to la Bawette, further to the north. Bülow was sent orders to move to Dion-le-Mont, south-east of Wavre. Once this movement was completed, the

Prussian army would have a chance to rest and lick its many wounds. Order could now be fully restored, although this would not be easy.

Napoleon's army too needed to rest and recuperate. In the confusion and darkness at the end of the battle, it had been impossible to organise an effective pursuit of the Prussians. Contact was more or less lost, although some cavalry patrols clashed with the Prussians. At daylight, further patrols were sent out. In the early hours of 17 June, two crucial points had yet to be clarified. Firstly, did Wellington intend to hold his position at Quatre Bras, or had he just left a rearguard there? Secondly, in which direction were the Prussians retreating? As the morning went on, reports came in. The fog of war slowly began to clear.

The first report from Quatre Bras arrived in Napoleon's headquarters at 7.30am. It indicated that Wellington had held his positions in the previous day's fighting and was bivouacking on the battlefield. A little later, news of the Prussians arrived. Cavalry patrols reported taking many prisoners from the mass of men fleeing eastwards, towards Liège and Namur. After that came news of the capture of Prussian artillery and baggage waggons, indications that they were in full flight. This gave Napoleon cause to believe he had now separated Blücher from Wellington. His strategy appeared to be working and there did not appear to be any urgent need to add to the plight of the Prussians by staging a close pursuit.

Around noon, Napoleon received a further report from cavalry moving on Gembloux that also indicated a withdrawal eastwards. Because of this, Napoleon did not send any patrols northwards, towards Wavre, and this error allowed the main body of the Prussians slip away. By now, Napoleon had already all but lost Waterloo, although it was too early for him to realise. He later blamed Grouchy for this state of affairs, but that was just a case of passing the blame.

Despite the news received, Napoleon had yet to fully discount the possibility that Blücher would nevertheless attempt to link up with Wellington. He needed to determine their intentions and, that afternoon, sent Grouchy on his way with nearly one-third of his entire army; the corps of Gérard and Vandamme, Teste's division and two cavalry corps. Grouchy's orders were to establish the intentions of both Wellington and Blücher. He would start by looking in the wrong place.

That afternoon, Grouchy's patrols located a strong force of Prussians, some 25,000 to 30,000 men in Gembloux. They also indicated that there were no Prussians in Namur. Grouchy reacted by ordering his forces on Gembloux, where Vandamme arrived about 7pm and Gérard three hours later. But the trail had gone cold, as Thielemann had slipped away at 2pm.

What added to Grouchy's difficulties was the torrential rain that fell that day. This restricted visibility and made it difficult to locate the Prussians. From Gembloux, Grouchy sent out patrols further east, to Sart-à-Walhain and Perwez. His troopers sought information on the Prussian movements and were told they might be going in the direction of Wavre. French scouts clashed with the Prussian rearguard at Tourinnes, confirming the suspicion that some Prussians were moving on Wavre. At 10pm, Grouchy reported the situation to Napoleon, explaining that he had now located two columns of Prussians, one moving on Wavre, the other on Namur. He then issued orders for his force to move to Sart-à-Walhain the coming morning. Once there, Grouchy would then decide in which direction to go – Wavre or Namur. He would not be in a position to cut off the Prussians from marching westwards to support Wellington.

The route, the features and the terrain
The countryside through which Gneisenau and Grouchy passed on 17 June is much the same today as it was then, at least until the motorway that now runs to the north of Mont St Guibert was built. Beyond that, and into Wavre, there is little that the soldiers of 1815 would recognise, as urbanisation and industrialisation have taken their toll. Most of these lanes would have been unmade in 1815, so it is fortunate indeed that the heavy rainfall did not start until later in the day, allowing the Prussians to make good progress. Had Grouchy's troopers caught them in that deluge, then the Prussians might well have been cut down in great numbers and lost much of their wheeled transport, preventing them from playing an effective role on 18 June.

Wavre itself bears little resemblance to the town of 1815. There is a plaque commemorating the fighting of 18/19 June on the modern bridge of Christ

Plaque on the Pont du Christ bridge in Wavre. It marks the fighting on 18 June 1815.

Arthur Wellesley, the Duke of Wellington (1769–1852)

Born in Dublin to an impoverished family of the Anglo-Irish aristocracy in the same year as Napoleon, Wellington's rise to fame was linked to that of his arch rival. Arthur Wesley, as he was then known, did not excel at school and his early military career showed little of what was to come. He first saw action as a brigade commander in 1794 in Flanders, but his brigade was withdrawn in 1795. A year later, he sailed for India as commander of the 33rd Foot. It was here that Arthur Wellesley, as he was now known, first gained fame and fortune. After the storming of Seringapatam and the death of Tipoo Sultan, Wellesley was made governor of Mysore. Promoted to major-general in 1802, he saw action again the next year in the Second Mahratta War. He then embarked for home, arriving in time for Nelson's victory at Trafalgar in October 1805. Britannia's rule of the waves may have been secured, but Napoleon's victory at Austerlitz that December made him master of central Europe. Wellesley spent much of the next two years in politics before being sent on an expedition to Copenhagen in autumn 1807. The next summer he was posted to Portugal and began the long campaign that not only played a major role in breaking Napoleon's hold over Europe, but also made Wellington famous throughout the Continent. So much has been written about the Peninsular Campaign that there is little point in saying much here other then to point out that Wellington never crossed swords with Napoleon in these years. In 1814, while Blücher was fighting his way into northern France, Wellington's infamous army was crossing the Pyrenees. After Napoleon's first abdication, Wellington was created a duke and took up the post of ambassador to France in Paris. In February 1815, Wellington arrived in Vienna to replace Castlereagh as British plenipotentiary at the Congress. While there, Napoleon escaped from Elba and Wellington was sent to command the Allied army in the Netherlands. Surprised at Quatre Bras on 17 June, he muddled his way on, coming into his element as the greatest tactical general of his era at Waterloo. After Napoleon's second abdication, Wellington remained in France until 1818 as commander-in-chief of the army of occupation. On his return to Britain, he renewed his career in politics, holding numerous posts in government and the army, including that of prime minister.

The Bierges mill, near Wavre. Bitter fighting also took place in and around this mill. As the previous day's torrential rain had swollen the Dyle river, the mill stood out like an island fortress in the flood.

that runs over the Dyle in the centre of the town. A few streets north of the bridge, down a turning to the right, is the church of Saint-Jean-Baptiste that has a cannonball embedded in the fourth pillar on the right, but one cannot be certain if this is battle damage or mere decoration. A little way further from the church, to the right, up the Haute Route de Bruxelles on the left, is the rue d'Escaile, where a hotel of the same name stands. This was a field hospital during the battle. Retracing

The Dyle river near the mill. Even when not flooded, this deep channel with its steep banks was a formidable obstacle.

one's steps and continuing to the Hôtel de Ville, one sees the former Carmelite convent that also served as a field hospital.

Downriver from the centre of town the solid Bierges mill is still standing, at the end of the rue de Manège. Held by a company of Prussian infantry on 18 June, it stood like a solid island of rock in the flooded Dyle valley. Gérard was wounded in the fighting around here, and there is a monument to him between the Boulevard de l'Europe and the mill.

One kilometre north of Wavre, on the N4, near the golf club, stands the Château de la Bawette, which housed Thielemann's headquarters during the battle.

While little of the original architecture remains, the topography of this area has not changed. The ground immediately south of Wavre, on the far side of the Dyle, is relatively flat. Any troops moving to attack the town would have to march downhill from Aisemont in the face of an artillery barrage. Today, the Dyle has been channelled and the marshes drained, but the deluge of 17 June made the river impassable, except over one of the few bridges that would, of course, be heavily defended. On the far side of the Dyle, the terrain rose sharply, providing good positions for the Prussian artillery. The hills north of Wavre were like great fortresses and the Dyle their moat. A small rearguard could hold up a large force here, so Grouchy would have enormous difficulty in taking this position. A small force of Prussians could delay him for hours, while the main body slipped away and the swollen Dyle would prevent Grouchy from intercepting that force. There would be no chance of him stopping Blücher from taking most of his men to Waterloo. Napoleon's only chance was to defeat Wellington before Blücher arrived and the same rain that held up Grouchy would delay Blücher, giving Napoleon a chance of victory.

Chapter Two

The Night in Wavre

The Prussians arrive in Wavre

We left the Prussian forces at the point where they had been ordered to rally in the area of Wavre. After a few hours rest in Mellery, Blücher transferred his headquarters to Wavre, where he arrived at 6am, having ridden through the cheering masses of soldiers on this route. Despite the defeat, spirits were high.

Thielemann had departed from the Sombreffe area early on 17 June and, not having been informed of the intended line of retreat, at first started to move towards Gembloux. French pickets observed their movements, reporting this back to headquarters. This information confirmed Napoleon's belief that the Prussians were heading eastwards.

Zieten was the first to arrive in Wavre, bivouacking as ordered in the village of Bierges. His men were exhausted and lacked all essentials. They now needed to rest, eat and prepare themselves for the next day's battle.

Pirch I was the next to arrive, reaching Wavre shortly after Zieten. Thielemann and Bülow took longer to reach their destinations, as they had lost contact for a while with army headquarters. Indeed, a line of communication was established between Thielemann and Bülow before one was established with Wavre. Bülow informed Thielemann that he was moving on Wavre and suggested that Thielemann do the same, as the army was apparently assembling there. They conferred on the routes they should take to avoid

Prussian Uhlan, 1815. The Prussian cavalry was in the throes of a major reorganisation when the war of 1815 broke out. As such, its performance left much to be desired.

crossing each other's paths. Thielemann marched via Walhain and Corbais, while Bülow took the route via Tourinnes to Corry-le-Grand.

At about 10am, contact between army headquarters and Bülow was re-established. It was then that Bülow received his orders to move to Dion-le-Mont. Half an hour later, he wrote to Thielemann informing him of this and of reports that a body of what had been taken to be Prussian soldiers were seen moving to his left. Actually, it was a brigade of dragoons from Exelmans' Cavalry Corps, but it failed to notice the Prussians.

Just before 11.30am, the French clashed with Pirch I's rearguard at Mellery. The sound of firing coming from the direction of Quatre Bras died down at around the same time, so it seemed that Napoleon was switching his attention from Wellington to Blücher.

Prussian Landwehr, 1815. Many of the troops raised in 1815 consisted of untried militia from provinces previously under French rule. Lacking clothing, equipment and arms, it is remarkable how this army remained intact after the defeat at Ligny on 16 June 1815.

Around midday, Gneisenau pondered his next move. He knew the whereabouts of Zieten and Pirch I, but he had yet to locate Thielemann and had yet to hear that his orders had reached Bülow. Wellington had requested him for support the following day at Waterloo, but contact had been lost with the Prussian ammunition trains, so Gneisenau could not be certain of resupplying his men. He could not yet confirm his intention to move at least two army corps to assist Wellington.

Half an hour later, the Prussian pickets around Gentinnes reported seeing a build-up of French forces, indicating that a serious pursuit was imminent. However, these forces then moved off in the direction of Genappe. By 2pm, Napoleon's pursuit of Wellington started in earnest, which further delayed his search for Blücher. The twenty-four hours Napoleon had gained by humbugging Wellington at the beginning of the campaign were slipping away.

Concerned that the French movements might interrupt his communications with Wellington, Gneisenau ordered Zieten at 3pm to ensure that the entire line of the Dyle was kept under observation and that contact with their allies was maintained.

FIELD MARSHAL GENERAL PRINCE GEBHARDT LEBERECHT BLÜCHER VON WAHLSTADT (1742–1819)

Blücher's military career began in 1758 as a cadet in a Swedish hussar squadron recruited in their German territories. In 1760, he joined the Prussian service after being taken prisoner by them, and fought in Belling's Regiment for the remainder of the Seven Years War. In 1773, he resigned from the army after a dispute with his king, Frederick the Great. In the same year, he married for the first time and started a family. When Frederick died in 1786, Blücher made efforts to be reappointed to the army and the next year he was made a major commanding a squadron of hussars. By 1790 he had risen to the rank of full colonel. The next year, his first wife died. When war with France broke out in 1792, Blücher itched to draw his sabre. He participated in the campaigns in the Rhineland from 1793 to 1795, fighting at the Battle of Kaiserslautern and in many other actions. Shortly after Prussia's withdrawal from the Revolutionary Wars in 1795, he married again. His second wife bore him no children. Blücher's frustration grew in the ensuing ten years of peace and his mental health began to suffer. A sense of relief overtook him when Prussia finally went to war with France in 1806, having sat on the fence too long the previous year. He led the cavalry at the Battle of Auerstedt that October, but made little headway against the determined squares of Frenchmen, flushed with their success at Auerstedt the previous year. Blücher's spirited retreat to Lübeck raised his public profile, and he ended the war as a prisoner, but with his honour intact. The humiliating peace that followed the Jena campaign weighed on Blücher so heavily that he had a mental breakdown. However, he was such a popular figurehead that he could not be removed from his office. Instead, he now had several chiefs-of-staff in succession, each de facto commander of the forces nominally under Blücher's control. His frustration grew when Prussia did not join Austria in the war of 1809, and a promotion to general of cavalry and a backdated pay increase did little to alleviate this.

An active member of the anti-French party, Blücher itched to draw his sabre again. The opportunity came with the destruction of Napoleon's army in Russia in 1812. Blücher was appointed commander-in-chief of the Army of Silesia in March 1813, and fought alongside the Russians at Lützen and Bautzen that spring. Austria joined the Allies over the summer and the campaign continued into the autumn, with Blücher's dramatic victory over Macdonald that August. The Army of Silesia's crossing of the Elbe River was one of the actions that precipitated the great battle at Leipzig in October. The combat at Möckern, near the city of Leipzig, included some of the most bitter fighting of the campaign. The Army of Silesia suffered heavy casualties, and Blücher was promoted to Field Marshal General. That winter, he was the first to take the war into France, crossing the Rhine at Kaub over the New Year. After several setbacks, he reached Paris, forcing Napoleon's abdication. His celebratory trip to London in the summer of 1814 was premature. Appointed commander-in-chief of the Prussian Army of the Lower Rhine in April 1815, his role at Ligny and Waterloo was again decisive in defeating Napoleon. His vigorous pursuit after Waterloo, his capture of several strategic fortresses in Northern France and his entry into Paris sealed Napoleon's fate for good. Blücher died on his estate in Silesia in 1819.

Napoleon sending off the Imperial Guard for its final assault on Wellington's centre on the evening of 18 June 1815. It was the defeat of the Imperial Guard that precipitated the flight of the French army.

About 5pm, the missing ammunition trains arrived in Wavre. Gneisenau knew that two of his corps were now in a condition to fight the next day. However, the two remaining corps had yet to be report their positions to him, and a message came in that indicated Wellington might be falling back all the way to Brussels. Gneisenau was still not in a position to confirm his ability to support Wellington the next day, assuming that the Duke was still intending to fight at Waterloo.

At 8pm, Thielemann's corps began to arrive at Wavre and moved through the town to its bivouac to the north, the rearguard coming up at 6am the following day. Bülow's lead elements had been coming to Dion-le-Mont all afternoon and it was well into the night before his exhausted rearguard arrived. By 10pm, he felt confident his whole corps would be available the next day and reported this to headquarters. Gneisenau was now certain he could meet his part of the bargain made with Wellington; he next needed confirmation of the Duke's intentions. This duly arrived just before midnight and all was now set for the Prussians to march to Waterloo.

The preparations for the march to Waterloo

Although Bülow's Corps was the furthest away from Waterloo, it was selected to lead the march. This was because it was by far the freshest: Zieten had been decimated, Pirch I had been badly bloodied and Thielemann, as the next freshest, was most suitable to use as the rearguard.

Bülow's men spent the night in the area from Dion-le-Mont down the road to Chaumont (now the N243). The Reserve Cavalry was at the point, bivouacking between Dion-le-Mont and Bonlez. Down the road behind them, on the left of the road, Hake rested in the area of Tout Vent, the artillery behind him, and Hiller remained further down the road near Chaumont. Losthin bivouacked around Corry. Ryssel was still on the move and was designated to be the rearguard.

At midnight, Bülow was ordered to march the next morning from Dion-le-Mont through Wavre and to continue in the direction of Chapelle-St-Lambert. If Wellington was not heavily engaged, Bülow was expected to deploy there under cover. If Wellington was heavily engaged, then Bülow was expected to attack the French. Pirch I was ordered to follow Bülow after breakfast. Zieten and Thielemann were likewise instructed to cook a meal and then be prepared to move off.

At 2am, Wellington received confirmation that the Prussians would march to his aid that morning. The distance separating the two armies was not great, but it would be hours before the Prussians finally did arrive.

FRIEDRICH WILHELM COUNT BÜLOW VON DENNEWITZ (1755–1816)

Bülow was born on the family estate of Falkenberg in East Prussia on 16 February 1755. Just after his thirteenth birthday, he joined the army, becoming a cadet officer in his brother's Berlin-based infantry regiment, Count Lottum's, coincidentally the thirteenth in the line. This does not seem to have brought young Bülow any bad luck, because he rose through the ranks, becoming an ensign in 1772 and a 2nd lieutenant in 1778. Bülow was a man of intellect, and he applied himself to the study of history, mathematics and geography. He was also a talented musician, which brought him into contact with the royal court, where he got to know the royal princes, including

Louis Ferdinand, who was also a musician. Bülow first saw action at the Battle of Leopold during the War of the Bavarian Succession, gaining a promotion to 1st lieutenant in 1786, the year of Frederick the Great's death. Four years later, he became a junior captain before becoming a full captain in 1793, just before he went to war with France for the first time.

As he was made governor of Prince Louis Ferdinand, Bülow had clearly been earmarked for higher affairs. He saw considerable action at the side of Prussia's popular prince, fighting at the Battle of Kaiserslautern as well as in numerous skirmishes during the withdrawal to the Rhine. On 17 July 1793, Bülow led the assault on the Zahlbach redoubt in the fortress of Mainz and was awarded the coveted 'Pour le Mérite' for protecting his charge, who was badly wounded.

Now a veteran, Bülow was promoted to major unattached in 1794, before being given command of the Fusilier Battalion Stutterheim (No.21) in November 1795. He had been offered a more amenable post as Louis Ferdinand's teacher, but wanted to be in active service. Although Prussia had withdrawn from the Revolutionary Wars through the Peace of Basle of

1795, many considered a further conflict with France merely a matter of time. In 1797, Bülow was given his first independent command, as commander of the newly-raised Fusilier Battalion No.24, part of the East Prussian Brigade. The fusiliers were at this time élite light infantry formations trained in the newest skirmish tactics of the period and armed with a specially designed musket. These battalions were the nurseries of not only the universal infantryman of the 19th century, but also of the general staff, as many of their officers went on to high staff positions and senior command.

When the anticipated war with France broke out in 1806, Bülow, by now a full colonel, was on his estate in East Prussia, so he avoided the catastrophic defeats of Jena and Auerstedt. His brigade joined the corps of Prussians under General L'Estocq, fighting at Waltersdorf on 5 February 1807, where he was wounded in the left arm. That April, he joined Blücher's Corps in Pomerania, where he commanded the Fusilier Battalion Schachtmeyer (No.24), before being appointed to command a brigade.

Following the end of the disastrous war of 1806/7 with France, Bülow was appointed to the Investigative Commission to examine the causes of the defeat. However, Blücher, now military governor of the province of Pomerania, had a nervous breakdown, making him incapable of carrying out his duties, so Bülow remained there, covering for Blücher. Bülow was rewarded with a promotion to major-general in 1808 and from then until the end of the Napoleonic Wars remained one of the leading figures in the struggle against France.

Blücher duly recovered from his illness, but his relationship with Bülow deteriorated. This affected Bülow's health and eventually Blücher got him transferred to other duties. Bülow took up his new duties as commander of the West Prussian Brigade in 1811. He did not get a field command in the Russian campaign of 1812, but was made governor of both East and West Prussia, putting him in command of the border with Russia, a post requiring considerable diplomatic skill once the pursuing Russians arrived.

In December 1812, Bülow was ordered to call up the reserves. Prussia had yet to commit herself to a continuation of the war of 1812, and left the door open for an alliance with Russia. Bülow's geographical position was crucial, and the more men he had to hand, the better his bargaining position. By January, an East and West Prussian Reserve Corps had been raised along the Vistula, with Bülow's organisational talents playing a major role in this.

King Frederick William III of Prussia finally joined forces with the Czar in February 1813. Bülow's troops moved westwards, in the wake of the *retreating French. Bülow's cavalry clashed with French forces under Prince Eugene at Möckern on 5 April, driving them further back. While a Prusso-Russian army fought Napoleon at Lützen at the beginning of May, Bülow ejected the French garrison from the nearby city of Halle. When the news of the Allied defeat reached him, he was compelled to withdraw, abandoning his gains.*

Bülow was then placed in charge of the defence of Berlin and set about mobilising all available forces. He saw off the first French attempt to capture the capital of Prussia at Luckau on 4 June 1813. That summer's armistice allowed him the opportunity to complete his preparations and he raised a substantial body of militia. By the end of the armistice, he had a full army corps under his command, although a substantial part of it was poorly trained, untried and ill-equipped Landwehr. The III Army Corps was allocated to the Army of the North under the command of the Crown Prince of Sweden, once Napoleon's Marshal Bernadotte.

That autumn, Napoleon made two further attempts to seize Berlin. The first, under Marshal Oudinot, was driven back in the rain at Grossbeeren on 23 August. For his role in this, Bülow was awarded the Iron Cross 1st Class. Marshal Ney led the second attempt, which suffered a similar fate at Dennewitz on 6 September. Bülow received numerous awards for this victory. His corps arrived towards the end of the decisive Battle of Leipzig that October, along with the remainder of the Army of the North. From there, Bülow's Corps marched to the Netherlands, expelling the French occupiers. In February 1814, his men crossed the French border, fighting several battles before Napoleon finally abdicated. Bülow was then made a count in recognition of the role he played.

Hardly had Bülow returned home to his estate in East Prussia when Napoleon escaped from exile on the Mediterranean island of Elba, starting the Hundred Days of 1815. Now a full general, Bülow hoped to be placed in command of the Prussian army forming on the Lower Rhine, but that was not to be. Political expediency and popular demand saw to it that Blücher received this role, but as he was no longer capable of carrying it out, Gneisenau was made his chief-of-staff and effectively commanded, albeit in Blücher's name. Bülow must have seen this as a slight, and the friction between him and Gneisenau almost had fatal consequences for the Allied cause.

Chapter Three

The Strategic Position

Where was Wellington?

During the night of 16/17 June, Wellington's cavalry arrived at Quatre Bras and took up its positions in the line. At 3am, the picket lines clashed briefly, but otherwise the night remained as peaceful as it could be after a battle. His army bivouacked on the field of battle and waited for dawn. The Duke now had about 40,000 men at his disposal and outnumbered Ney, so his intention was to go over to the offensive that day, had Blücher held his positions. Indeed, Wellington issued orders to the remainder of his army that night to close in on Quatre Bras, so that he could do so.

A line of communication between the two headquarters had been set up that day and regular reports on the situation were both sent and received. The last Wellington had heard from the Prussians was that they were holding their own, and expected to do so for the remainder of the day. This message, timed at 7pm, arrived at Quatre Bras at 8.30pm. What Wellington did not know was that the French had intercepted the messenger that bore news of the Prussian retreat. It would be hours before he established the true situation at Ligny.

The next morning, Wellington returned to the battlefield. Having heard nothing from Blücher, he sent out patrols to re-establish contact. These patrols carefully avoided the French pickets before establishing contact with the rearguard of the Prussians. As it was some time before this information reached Wellington, the Duke started considering his options, deciding to fall back on Waterloo should the Prussians have been beaten. Confirmation of their defeat finally arrived at 7.30am. As Napoleon showed little sign of activity, Wellington was in no rush to depart, so he allowed his men to cook a meal before starting to move off.

At 8am, contact with the Prussian headquarters was re-established, when an officer brought news from Gneisenau. He informed Wellington of Gneisenau's intention of returning to the offensive once his men had been fed and resupplied. As that would take a day at least, Wellington did not change his decision to fall back. He asked the Prussian officer to pass on the news of his intention to offer a battle at Waterloo on 18 June should the Prussians agree to support him with two corps. Failing that, he would fall back to the fortress port of Antwerp, abandoning Brussels to the French. The Prussian officer departed for Wavre.

LIEUTENANT-GENERAL AUGUST WILHELM ANTON COUNT NEIDHARDT VON GNEISENAU (1760-1831)

Gneisenau's military career began in 1778 as a hussar in the Austrian army. A year later, he transferred to the Ansbach Jäger (riflemen) as a cadet. In 1782, he went to America but did not see action in the American War of Independence. After his return, he applied to Frederick the Great to join the Prussian army and was commissioned as a 2nd lieutenant in 1786. Gneisenau served in one of the newly founded 'free regiments', light infantry formations that later became the élite fusiliers. He first saw action in the partition of Poland in 1794, getting his own company a year later. In the 1806 campaign, Gneisenau was commended for his role in the Battle of Saalfeld and served at Jena on the staff of General von Rüchel. Gneisenau's first opportunity for fame came when he was appointed as commandant of the fortress of Kolberg, on the Baltic coast of Pomerania. This was the one Prussian fortress in the entire campaign that did not capitulate. Now in the limelight, Gneisenau went on to play a leading role in the military reforms that came in the following years. In 1809/10, he went on various diplomatic missions before rejoining the army early in 1813, becoming Blücher's chief-of-staff after Scharnhorst's mortal wounding at Lützen in May. From here onwards, Gneisenau fought at Blücher's side until the final overthrow of Napoleon after Waterloo. Due to his instability, Blücher held command in name only, and the actual leadership of the Army of Silesia and the Army of the Lower Rhine fell on Gneisenau's shoulders. After Waterloo, Gneisenau rose to the rank of field marshal and commanded the army that sealed off the border with Poland in 1831. He died that year of cholera.

Wellington then started issuing orders for the move to Waterloo. He not only those instructed troops at Quatre Bras to fall back, but he also directed those divisions at Nivelles to Waterloo. This movement commenced at 10am and was not subject to any interference. Byng and Picton were the first to march off, with Perponcher and Merlen following. Alten covered the rear and various battalions were deployed in vantage points along the route. Shortly before midday, the cavalry replaced the infantry outposts. While Alten withdrew via Genappe up the main road to Brussels, other units took the road running through Baisy. The Brunswick light infantry and the light companies of the British guard plugged the bottleneck in Genappe.

Meanwhile, three columns of cavalry covered the retreat, the left consisting of Dörnberg and Grant's brigades, the centre of Ponsonby and Somerset's heavy cavalry, the right of Vandeleur and Vivian's brigades. Napoleon attempted to delay this movement by opening up with his artillery, but did not succeed.

About 2pm, the torrential rain started, delaying all movement. The centre column of the Allied cavalry crossed the Dyle at Genappe before the French caught up with them. The pickets clashed, but once Uxbridge had withdrawn his troopers from Genappe, Napoleon did not pursue any further. (It is certainly worth taking the detour off the bypass and going to look at Genappe. While the town has changed since 1815, the impression given by the bridge and narrow streets indicates what a bottleneck this was. It delayed both Napoleon's advance to Waterloo and his retreat from it.)

Wellington continued from Genappe past le Maison du Roi and the farm of la Belle Alliance and on to Mont St Jean, where he halted. His men spent that evening and night bivouacked on what was to be the next day's battlefield, soaked to the skin and without shelter. Vivian covered the far left with a picket in Smohain. Next to him stood Vandeleur, while Saxe-Weimar's Nassauers took up positions inside the farmhouses of Papelotte, la Haye and Smohain. This force was to hold the left flank, anticipating the Prussian arrival here. Picton drew up along the ridge east of the Brussels to Charleroi road, with his right on the crossroads north of la Haye Sainte. Bijlandt's Netherlanders stood in front of him. Alten stood next to Picton, west of the highway. One battalion of KGL occupied the farm of la Haye Sainte. Continuing Wellington's line westwards was Cooke's division. Some of his men were sent to garrison the great château of Goumont, or Hougoumont as it is often known. Chassé secured Braine l'Alleud. Uxbridge's troopers were used to secure the flanks and held in reserve behind the main position.

Wellington's plan was very simple. He would hold his positions for as long as possible, preferably until the Prussians arrived. That would, however, be much later than he at first anticipated.

Where was Napoleon?

Napoleon followed up, taking up positions around la Belle Alliance, on the ridge opposite Mont St Jean. D'Erlon was in the front line, between the Mon-Plaisir farm south-west of Hougoumont and Plancenoit. Jacquinot's cavalry covered his front line. In the second line stood Milhaud's cuirassiers, Domon's light cavalry, Subervie and the Guard Cavalry. They bivouacked along the Rossomme heights, south of la Belle Alliance. Reille, Lobau and Kellermann remained in the area around Genappe. The baggage trains blocked the main road, so the Guard was diverted. Much delayed, it finally reached the village of Glabais by midnight, having taken a circuitous route. Napoleon set up his headquarters in the farm of le Caillou, near the Charleroi road, where there is now a museum. In the garden is a small ossuary and a monument to the 1st Battalion of the 1st Chasseurs of the Imperial Guard can be seen in the farm orchard. Down the east fork at the junction just south of le Caillou is the road that leads to the farm of Chantelet, where Ney spent the night before the battle.

Chantelet farm. Marshal Michel Ney spent the night before the battle here.

MARSHAL GEORGES MOUTON COUNT DE LOBAU (1770–1813)

Lobau too volunteered for the army in the Revolutionary Wars and rose through the ranks, fighting in France and in the Rhineland. In 1796, he was sent to Italy, serving at the siege of Mantua and in various subsequent actions. In 1805 he was made a general, and as an ADC to Napoleon fought at Austerlitz and then at Jena in 1806, before being severely wounded at Friedland in 1807. Later that year, he was promoted to a divisional general. In 1808, he was sent to Spain, serving in Soult's Corps. In 1809, he was transferred to Bavaria, fighting at Abensberg, Landshut and Eckmühl before covering himself with glory at Aspern-Essling, covering the retreat to the island of Lobau. Made a count for his deeds that day, he was wounded at Wagram a few weeks later. He participated in the Russian campaign in 1812 as a senior aide to Napoleon, accompanying him back to Paris that December. He fought at Lützen in the spring of 1813, and at Dresden that autumn, where he was taken prisoner. He returned to France after Napoleon's first abdication. After serving under Louis XVIII, he rejoined Napoleon for the Hundred Days, fighting at Ligny on 16 June and in the action at Plancenoit on 18 June. He then went to England, but was allowed to return to France in December 1818, where he went into politics. He broke up a Bonapartist demonstration in 1831 and died in 1838 from an old wound.

What did Blücher need to achieve?

Napoleon outnumbered and outgunned Wellington, whose army consisted in part of inexperienced and unreliable troops. Nobody was sure how long Wellington could hold out against him, so speed was of the essence to be sure of victory. The Prussians certainly started on their way early enough, and had all gone well, they could have arrived in the late morning or early afternoon. As we will see, they were delayed by a combination of circumstances beyond their control. The clock was ticking in Napoleon's favour.

Chapter Four

The March to Plancenoit

The terrain, features and locations

The terrain between Dion-le-Mont and Chapelle-St-Lambert was hilly, with a number of steep slopes, and was scored by a number of ridges and ravines. The first bottleneck was the crossing of the Dyle at Wavre. Once on the far side, Bülow would have to pass through the narrow streets of the town, before taking the unmade lanes through Bierges and Rixensart to Chapelle-St-Lambert. The distance the furthest part of his corps would have to march was 25km from Vieux-Sart to Plancenoit. It was 21km to the Paris Wood, where he made his first halt, and Vieux-Sart is 8km from Wavre. The distance from Wavre to Chapelle-St-Lambert was 10km. It was a further 3km from Chapelle-St-Lambert to the Paris Wood. In normal conditions, good troops could be expected to cover that distance in six hours. When rushing to aid an ally in need of urgent assistance, less time than that should have been taken. In fact, Bülow took eleven hours to assemble his men at the designated point. Why was that?

The church at St Lambert. Having made a gruelling march in deep mud from Wavre, Bülow's Corps rested here for several hours before making its advance to Plancenoit.

Bülow's march to Plancenoit

Losthin was first to set off that morning, followed by Hiller, then Hake, then the artillery, then the cavalry and finally Ryssel, who brought up the rear. Bülow saw to it that the accompanying wheeled transport was kept to a minimum. The march began at daybreak, but the late arrival of the supply trains meant that his men went off to face battle without having a cooked meal inside them.

There were delays in getting Losthin's baggage trains on the move, which delayed Hiller's start until 6am. One delay always causes the next, and it was 9am before the cavalry could start off. Obviously, the rearguard could only move off when the rest of the corps was on its way, and it did so at 10am, after having been in the saddle for six hours. Just as it did, Exelmans' vanguard engaged Ryssel and he was forced to leave behind two regiments of cavalry to hold off this threat.

The Town Hall in Wavre. A Carmelite convent in 1815, it served as a hospital during the Battle of Wavre.

The most direct route to the field of Waterloo was on the right bank of the Dyle, which could be crossed at various places upriver. However, this would leave the corps open to attacks from the pursuing French, so Bülow had to cross the river at Wavre and use the marshy course of the Dyle to cover his left while en route. There was just one bridge there, which caused a further delay.

Bülow started his march through Wavre at 7am. Once over the bridge, the many vehicles inside the town blocked the streets. As Wavre was the site of the army headquarters, many of the baggage trains were parked there. Also, the field hospitals with their associated traffic were in the centre of town, exacerbating the problem. It is not surprising that a major traffic jam took place in Wavre, delaying the movement. Then there was a steep uphill climb through the crowded town along roads made slippery by the deluge of the previous day. A broken-down twelve-pound cannon blocked the road for a short while before it was removed. The delays did not stop there.

Losthin's Brigade exited Wavre just as a fire broke out in the town. Powder waggons were trying to pass through the narrow streets, and their proximity led to a panic. Some rushed out of the town, while others tried to retrace their steps back across the bridge, which was of course being crossed by the troops behind. Chaos ensued and fortunately a company of sappers, aided by others, soon got the flames under control, but not before there had been a further delay. This hold-up passed all the way down the line. Pirch I's men had to stand around waiting as well. Losthin halted for a while, allowing the remainder of the corps to catch up.

Once out of Wavre, more delays were to come. Having wound its way through the narrow, crooked streets of Wavre, Bierges and Limal, the route led uphill. Thanks to the heavy rain, the paths had turned into a quagmire. The guns had to be dragged uphill on tow ropes, tiring out the men before they had even reached the field of battle. Once the wheeled vehicles had been pulled to the top of a hill, great exertions were needed to stop them sliding down the mudchutes on the far side and getting damaged. While the cavalry and infantry made fair progress, the artillery literally got stuck in the mud. The twelve-pounder battery with the vanguard was abandoned.

At 9am, Losthin started to arrive at St Lambert. It took a couple of hours for his brigade to assemble there. His patrols pushed on to the far side of the Paris Wood, where at 10am Wellington observed them. About midday, Losthin's assembly was complete, and two battalions were sent into the Paris Wood. Once they had worked their way through to the far side, the main body of the brigade deployed, forming up into two lines behind

MAJOR-GENERAL GEORG DUBISLAV LUDWIG VON PIRCH I (1763–1838)

Pirch's military career began in 1775 as a cadet in a Prussian infantry regiment. He participated in the campaign in the Netherlands in 1787 and next saw action in the siege of Mainz in 1793. After Jena in 1806, he spent two years as a prisoner-of-war in France. In April 1813, he was appointed brigade commander, and fought as part of Kleist's II Army Corps, part of the Army of Bohemia at Lützen, Bautzen, Dresden, Kulm and Leipzig. In 1814, he was present at the Battle of Laon, fighting under Blücher. Circumstances in 1815 projected Pirch to command an army corps. General Borstell, commander of the II Army Corps, protested about the rough handling of the Saxon contingent after their rebellion against the Prussians in May 1815 and was sent home. Pirch was placed in command of the corps in his place, but was somewhat out of his depth. After fighting at Ligny and Waterloo, Pirch passed on his corps to Prince August of Prussia, who then commanded it for the remainder of the campaign. His brother, also a major-general, commanded a brigade in Zieten's Corps in 1815. The designation 'I' indicated his seniority over an officer of the same name and rank.

the Wood. The final part of the march from Chapelle-St-Lambert to Fichermont proved the most difficult. The ground dropped sharply into the Lasne valley. Once the guns had been manhandled all the way down this side of the valley, they then had to be dragged all the way up the other side. A handful of French troops in the area could have fixed the Prussians at this point for hours, but Napoleon's mind was elsewhere.

At noon, Wellington's staff officers held a conference with their Prussian counterparts. They were informed that the Prussian intervention would become effective at about 4pm. Wellington now knew that he had to hold his position until then and he advised Bülow to remain at St Lambert until it had been established that Napoleon posed no threat to his left flank. Cavalry patrols were sent off to reconnoitre the area.

An hour later, an unexpected movement to his right attracted Napoleon's attention. A body of troops was seen in the distance, about 9km away, on the heights of St Lambert. At that distance, it was difficult to be certain who they were, but as they could not be French, they could only be Prussians. A message was written to Grouchy urging him to interdict any Prussian move against Napoleon's right. Before it could be sent, a Prussian courier was captured. He was carrying the news that Bülow was intending to attack Napoleon's right flank, so a postscript was added to the message to Grouchy instructing him to move to join Napoleon. By now, it was simply too late for him to do so and Napoleon knew this.

Lobau was ordered to move to face the Prussians. His two divisions of cavalry under Subervie and Domon moved towards the Paris Wood. His two divisions of infantry, under Simmer and Jeanin, followed shortly afterwards.

Hiller moved up to Chapelle-St-Lambert at 2pm, having reached the heights of St Lambert at 11.30am. Ryssel arrived at about 3pm. It had taken Bülow six hours to concentrate in his assembly area. He was now ready to go over to the offensive.

Zieten's march to Fichermont

Although Zieten took a different route to Waterloo, it was no less treacherous. At midnight on 17/18 June, Zieten was sent his orders for the coming day. He was instructed to cook breakfast early and be prepared to move off after having eaten. This was the first warm food his men had eaten since the start of the campaign. While waiting for the order to move off, Zieten's men took the opportunity to clean their muskets and replenish their ammunition. After three days of constant fighting and marching – Zieten had done more of that than anybody else in the campaign so far – this was a welcome, if short-lived, respite.

Around noon, the order to move off was given. While Bülow and Pirch I were already on their way to attack Napoleon's right flank, Zieten was to move further to the north and link up with Wellington's left. That morning's events in and around Wavre had caused considerable delays already, so when Zieten started his march from Bierges, he crossed paths with Pirch I. As Pirch I was waiting for the road in front of him to clear, so he could continue his march, Zieten took the opportunity of taking his leading brigade through to the Froidmont road. However, Pirch I then started off, so the remainder of Zieten's men had to wait until he was out of the way. Zieten's vanguard moved off at 1pm and reached the battlefield well before the remainder of the corps. His rearguard spent much of the afternoon in Bierges.

LIEUTENANT-GENERAL WIEPRECHT HANS KARL FRIEDRICH ERNST HEINRICH COUNT VON ZIETEN (1770–1848)

Coming from one of the leading families of Brandenburg and related to Frederick the Great's famous hussar general, Zieten joined the hussar regiment bearing his family's name as a cadet in 1785. He first saw action in the Revolutionary Wars, participating in the Cannonade of Valmy in 1792. In 1806, he fought at Auerstedt. In the following years, he rose through the ranks, and was given his own hussar regiment in 1808. He next saw action in May 1813 as a brigade commander at Lützen. That autumn, Zieten fought in several major battles, including Dresden, Kulm and Leipzig. He was part of the army that invaded France in 1814. His role as commander of the rearguard action on 15 June 1815 played a significant part in the Allied victory in the Waterloo Campaign, as did his determined defence of St Amand and Ligny the next day. His corps was decimated in those two days, yet it pulled itself together again, reaching Waterloo on 18 June. Zieten's timely arrival allowed Wellington to draw forces from his left flank to his centre just in time to meet Napoleon's final attack. This was a further significant contribution to the Allied victory.

From Froidmont, Zieten's route ran via Ohain, in the valley of the Smohain brook. This brook ran from the Papelotte farm. The vanguard consisted of the 1st Brigade and the corps cavalry, followed by the three remaining brigades with the corps artillery at the rear. Zieten was aware he would have to deploy into battle order quickly, so he ordered his men wherever possible to march by divisions and not sections. Like the route taken by Bülow and Pirch I, this one was equally difficult, being cut by defiles and valleys. The soil was a heavy lime that the recent rain had turned into a quagmire that clogged wheels and axles and pulled off footwear. Zieten worked his way through this obstacle course and his point, a regiment of hussars, reached Ohain just before 6pm, where they linked up with Wellington's left. The Duke could now take men from here to reinforce his battered centre just before Napoleon's final assault.

Bülow closes on Plancenoit

We left Bülow in his assembly area at St Lambert. While waiting for the rear elements, and particularly the artillery, to move up, cavalry patrols were sent out to scout the terrain and determine Napoleon's dispositions to the south and west. These patrols went southwards towards Maransart, Céroux and Mont St Guibert to determine whether Grouchy was in a position to intercept Bülow and take him in the flank, while he attacked Napoleon. Pickets spread out between the Lasne and the Dyle.

The patrol sent to Mont St Guibert detected French activity from 9am onwards, when small groups of cavalry were observed. Scouts were sent out to learn more and there were a few minor clashes. Nothing indicated a major French thrust in the area, but the prisoners taken indicated that Grouchy had sent them to link up with Napoleon.

The patrol sent to Céroux did not find any French activity there. It continued to la Hutte and from there, on to les Flamandes, near to the Brussels to Charleroi highway and deep in Napoleon's rear. This patrol took a handful of foraging French soldiers prisoner, who informed their captors that Napoleon was engaged with Wellington and had taken his Guard with him. It was now clear that there was no threat to Bülow's left flank. After reporting this to headquarters, the patrol then passed through Maransart, moving back to Bülow's main position. From this hill, the Prussian cavalry could observe Napoleon's positions, which spread as far as Fichermont. This too was reported back to headquarters. Finally, this patrol rode back to the Brussels highway, reaching it at Passe-Avant, south of le Caillou. The Prussians were moving about in Napoleon's rear, freely and unchallenged.

Meanwhile, to the north, some of Bülow's staff officers were out scouting the terrain west of St Lambert, the route the corps would take to join the battle. There were rises and dips transecting the route and bushes running along a line of heights that reached as far as the Paris Wood blocked part of it.

A further patrol reached the Paris Wood after 9am. There was no French activity here either, and the movements of both Napoleon's and Wellington's armies could be seen in the distance. This patrol then rode on to Smohain, where it met a patrol of the British 10th Hussars. The news that Bülow was at St Lambert and on his way was dispatched to Wellington immediately. Blücher and Wellington had started to link their forces before the battle had begun.

Napoleon had done absolutely nothing to prevent the union of the two Allied armies. The earlier gains he had made were now slipping away. In such broken terrain, just a few well-positioned men could have delayed the Prussian advance. There were several suitable places to deploy them, including the defile of the Lasne brook, or the Paris Wood, but these crucial chokepoints were left to the Prussians. It would now be impossible to stop them joining the coming battle.

Now that contact was established, a line of communication was set up between Wellington and Blücher. From 10am onwards, the Duke was aware of every Prussian move. Indeed, he observed bodies of Prussian troops in the distance at about that time. An hour later, Blücher arrived at Chapelle-St-Lambert.

Shortly before noon, a conference between some of Wellington and Blücher's staff officers was held, in which the plans for that day were discussed. Three possibilities were considered. Firstly, if Napoleon were to attack Wellington's right, the Prussian army should move via Ohain to join him. Secondly, if Napoleon were to attack Wellington's centre and left, the Prussians were to advance on Napoleon's right. Finally, if Napoleon turned to face the Prussians at St Lambert, Wellington would advance against his left flank and rear. In the event, it was the second scenario that took place.

The time that the Prussian advance could be expected to take effect was also discussed. Wellington was aware that two of Bülow's brigades had reached St Lambert by 11.30am, but that it would be 4pm before the entire corps was concentrated for battle, with the artillery coming up last. Just after the Battle of Waterloo had started, the Allies had decided on their plan of action and Wellington was aware almost to the minute of how long he would have to hold out until Bülow could join him.

Aided by a local farmer, Bülow's chief-of-staff Valentini now selected the route for the final stage of the approach to the battlefield. The farmer took Valentini to a route that led through the Paris Wood. The Prussians were pleased to find there were no French here, as even a small number of men could have caused considerable problems. On the far side of the wood, the Prussians observed French flankers, as cavalry detachments on a field of battle were known. These flankers were so preoccupied with the events to their fore that they did not notice the arrival of the Prussians, who quickly secured their prize.

Having now taken control of the Paris Wood, the Prussians had a platform from which they could launch their attack on Napoleon's right. From here, the broken terrain opened out into a plateau that led from the wood to the village of Plancenoit, about 2.5km away. The Prussians could now deploy into battle formation out of the range of the French artillery.

Bülow's leading units took a rest, while the wheeled transport and artillery came up. In the following three or so hours, Prussian staff officers were able to observe the battle through their telescopes.

Meanwhile, strenuous efforts were undertaken to bring up the guns. A good impression of what the Prussians faced can be obtained from the Château de la Kelle, opposite the village of Lasne at the top of the eastern

The Kelle Farm. A little further down the road on this side of the farm is the slope that caused the Prussian artillery so many problems on 18 June 1815. It was then a mudchute, but today it has been paved over.

bank of the Lasne brook. The road down into the valley was a mudchute that day, and care had to be taken getting them down the valley side. The narrow Lasne valley was carrying the heavy rain of the previous day and had turned into a bog. The guns sank up to their axles and had to be hauled out, exhausting their crews before they had even reached the battlefield. If that was not enough, the guns had then to be hauled up the far side of the valley. Blücher, now recovered from the injuries sustained on 16 June, was seen everywhere, urging on his men, but precious time was lost. It was now 3pm.

All this time, the Prussian staff officers looked around nervously, waiting for the French to notice them and interrupt their movement at so critical a phase. A picket line was thrown out to prevent the French taking the Prussians by surprise, but fortunately Napoleon did not pay any attention to Bülow's men. He was gambling on winning the battle against Wellington before the Prussians could become effectively involved. At about this time, Napoleon received a message from Grouchy, timed at 11.30am, which indicated Grouchy was then about 20km from Wavre and had not established what Prussian forces might be to his left, that is, between him and Napoleon. Grouchy was in Walhain when he sent this report and it was clear to Napoleon that his marshal would not be in a position to join him at Waterloo that day. Time was running out. What is

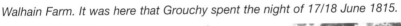

Walhain Farm. It was here that Grouchy spent the night of 17/18 June 1815.

more, although Napoleon still had infantry reserves available to throw against Wellington, he would have to think twice about committing them in case he needed men to hold off the advancing Prussians. The Prussian intervention was taking effect.

Bülow's brigades moved on towards the battlefield. At about 3pm, Losthin arrived at the Paris Wood. Shortly afterwards, his cavalry screen clashed with a French patrol, and Colonel Count Schwerin was killed. He was likely to have been the first Prussian officer killed in the battle and a monument to him can be seen on the road that skirts the northern edge of the Paris Wood. Hiller followed Losthin, reaching the village of Lasne at 3.30pm. The cavalry came up next, having passed through Hake to get to the front. Once through the Lasne defile, at about 4pm, the cavalry drew up behind Hiller. After three hours resting at Chapelle-St-Lambert, Hake marched off at 2.45pm, passing through the defile and arriving at Lasne an hour later. After a short rest, the march continued, with Hake reaching the Paris Wood around 4.30pm. Next, around 5pm, came the mud-caked artillery, having trailed its way from St Lambert, holding up Ryssel all the time. He finally reached the battlefield at about 5.30pm. By the time the last of Bülow's men reached the battlefield, the first were already engaged in combat.

The current owner of the Walhain farm was kind enough to produce this plaque from his barn. The building is undergoing renovations and the plaque will be reattached to the wall in due course.

Chapter Five

Plancenoit

The village, the features and the terrain

The plateau onto which Bülow's men were deploying ran directly towards the village of Plancenoit. At that point, the ground rose gently, with the village being on a mound. A ravine ran around the east and south of the village. On the near side of the ravine, to the north-east, was a copse. The main road from the north ran into a gully. The Prussian war memorial stands here.

The houses were solid little buildings, most with cellars and ideal for defence, although unlike at Hougoumont, la Haye Sainte and Papelotte, little had been done to prepare them. Crowning the mound was the village church, surrounded by a stout wall. (The building there today, the church of St Antoine, dates from 1856. On the wall outside the main door is a bronze plaque to the Young Guard. Inside the church on the left, near the altar, there is a plaque to Lt Tattet.) In 1815, the church was like a citadel, while the houses served as the walls of this fortress-like village.

The visitor is recommended to take a walk around the centre of the village and take in the atmosphere. From the edge of the village, the view

The view towards Plancenoit. This is how the advancing Prussians would have seen their objective – the church spire is just visible and would have served as a marker. Behind them was the Bois de Paris and to the right, Fichermont.

Church Spire

The view from Plancenoit to the north-east. The French troops occupying Plancenoit would have seen the Prussians advancing over this terrain.

to the east will give a good idea of what Napoleon's men saw coming towards them on that fateful afternoon.

The Lasne brook had cut a steep ravine south of Plancenoit and there was a wood covering the steep rise on the far side. This terrain would impede Prussian attempts to circumvent the village from the south.

In all, this was a strong position and one that would prove both difficult to take and, once captured, just as difficult to hold. Had Napoleon prepared it properly for the defence, it would have been all the more difficult for the Prussians to capture.

The tactical situation

As we have seen, Napoleon first observed the Prussian movement around 1pm, yet he did not undertake any measures to bottle up Bülow's men in the Paris Wood. Around 3.30pm, a French patrol clashed with the Prussians and Napoleon was now faced with an imminent assault from the Prussians on his right rear. Opposing them, he had the cavalry divisions of Domon and Subervie, with Lobau's two infantry divisions in support. The Guard was the only reserve he had left and it was standing near Plancenoit. Two of d'Erlon's divisions, Durette's infantry and Jacquinot's cavalry, were engaged with the troops holding Wellington's left, Nassauers under the Prince of Saxe-Weimar.

Meanwhile, Wellington's right centre was suffering the first of several massed cavalry assaults under the leadership of Marshal Ney. The assaults

44

The Château of Papelotte. Held by Nassau troops that day, this building was badly damaged during the day's fighting.

Farm of Papelotte, 1825. Restoration work started soon after the battle and this fine building was restored to its former glory.

continued for several hours, significantly weakening Wellington's army and drawing in ever more of his reserves. Napoleon could not use his infantry reserves to support his cavalry, as the appearance of the Prussians on his right had tied them down.

Bülow was concentrating his men for the coming battle, waiting for his much delayed reserve artillery to come up. A request for urgent assistance then arrived from Wellington. Just as it did, one of his batteries on the Duke's left was seen to limber up and retire. This was taken as a sign that his position was crumbling, so Blücher instructed a reluctant Bülow to throw in the two brigades he had to hand, without waiting for his reserve artillery to arrive. A Prussian battery attached to one of the brigades then unlimbered and fired at Domon's troopers, driving them back. The sounds of the Prussian guns indicated to Wellington that the Prussian intervention had now begun in earnest. The battle for Plancenoit was about to begin.

The advance on Plancenoit

Only the two leading brigades of Bülow's Corps, Losthin and Hiller, were available for this first assault on Plancenoit. Losthin deployed north of the road leading to Plancenoit, Hiller to the south. Two of Losthin's battalions were detached and sent to link up with Saxe-Weimar, who was in danger of losing his hold on his positions. Two of Hiller's battalions were sent south, towards the Lasne. Two regiments of cavalry drew up in front of the two brigades. The brigades deployed into battle formation, the fusilier battalions to the fore, ready to open out into skirmish order. Two waves of assault columns drew up behind them. Two divisions of French cavalry waited for them, with two divisions of infantry standing behind them, one each side of the highest point of Plancenoit road. The ground sloped down gently towards the advancing Prussians.

It was now past 4pm. The Prussians could see the tip of the spire of the church in Plancenoit, which served as a marker for their line of advance. They could also see the great waves of French cavalry charging into Wellington's depleted and crumbling squares. At this crucial moment, they would make their presence felt.

The Prussian assault commenced around 4.30pm. First to engage the French were the two battalions detached from Losthin's brigade. They reached the château of Fichermont and, finding it occupied by the French, deployed their skirmish platoons. A determined bayonet charge cleared the buildings of their occupiers. Prussian hussars threw back a regiment of French cavalry, but a counterattack from their reserve repelled the Prussians. More Prussian cavalry came up, restoring the situation, and the Prussians now linked up with Wellington's army. Napoleon's slim hold on victory was slipping away.

LIEUTENANT-GENERAL JOHANN ADOLF VON THIELEMANN (1765–1824)

Thielemann joined the Saxon army in 1780 as a cadet. As a cavalryman, he participated in the Revolutionary Wars, fighting in several actions. In 1806 he fought at Jena and afterwards was involved in the peace negotiations between Napoleon and the Prince Elector of Saxony. In 1807, he participated in the siege of Danzig and later fought at Friedland. In 1809 he commanded the corps sent against the uprising in Germany led by the Duke of Brunswick. In 1812 he led a cavalry brigade at the Battle of Borodino, for which he was made a baron. In February 1813, he was appointed governor of the important fortress city of Torgau, strategically situated on the Elbe river. While the King of Saxony pondered which side to take in the coming war, Thielemann pressed him to join the Allies. When, in May 1813, he was ordered to hand it over to the French, Thielemann dutifully obeyed, then resigned his commission and joined the Russian army. That autumn, he led a raiding party consisting of Russian, Austrian and Prussian cavalry, fighting in numerous actions across Germany and into the Netherlands. At the end of the campaign of 1814 he was placed in command of the III German Army Corps on the Lower Rhine. In March 1815 he transferred to the Prussian service, and was placed in the unenviable position of being a Saxon in a senior position in the Prussian army during his countrymen's rebellion against the Prussians. Although not heavily committed at Ligny on 16 June, he held off Grouchy's pursuit at Wavre on 18/19 June, preventing this force from becoming involved at Waterloo. He remained in Prussian service until his retirement.

Losthin now pressed forward, up the ridge to where Jeanin was waiting to meet him. Lobau, perceiving his flanks to be threatened, pulled back. His cavalry held off the advancing Prussians long enough for his infantry to fall back as far as Plancenoit. One brigade occupied the village. The others turned to face front again, taking up positions to the north of Plancenoit, with the support of Lobau's cavalry and artillery. The Prussians brought up their artillery to the crest of the ridge they had just taken. With his right flank secure on Plancenoit, Lobau now had a position he could hold. Just two brigades of Prussians were not going to make much headway, so Bülow brought up more men. The battle for Plancenoit was now going to become a slogging match, but Napoleon had been deprived of the reserves he needed to win the battle for Wellington's centre. The Prussian advance had by now certainly begun to take effect, but it would be hours yet before they took control of Plancenoit.

Zieten comes up

While Bülow brought up more men to assault Plancenoit, Zieten linked up with Wellington's left. He had ordered his men to march to Ohain via Froidmont, but they went too far north, taking the route via Genval instead. This caused some delay and separated Zieten from Bülow. The terrain and condition of the roads added to the hold-ups. The path along which Steinmetz, the corps' vanguard, moved was in such poor condition that his infantry had to march in files. They had to spread out so much that all semblance of order was lost. For once, the artillery was not the slowest, and it kept up with the cavalry at the point of Steinmetz's brigade. From Genval, Zieten marched south and Steinmetz reached the Lasne defile about 5pm. Here it halted to reform its ranks and to allow Pirch II to catch up.

Meanwhile, Zieten's chief-of-staff Reiche continued towards the field of battle, where he met Müffling. Müffling had ridden to Wellington's left to establish the positions and intentions of his countrymen. The two men conferred, with Müffling telling Reiche that Wellington's situation was desperate, and that Blücher's army needed to intervene immediately to prevent his line from collapsing. Reiche rode back to his corps only to find that Zieten had left Steinmetz and ridden to the rear to hurry on the movement. Reiche then took the cavalry from the vanguard and rushed to join Wellington's positions. Steinmetz's cavalry were the first Prussians to contact Wellington's left, this being around 6pm. Vivian then moved his cavalry to Wellington's centre, later followed by other troops, so the Duke was now certainly aware that the Prussian advance had taken effect.

Zieten's remaining brigades followed. Meanwhile, more of Bülow's brigades drew up in front of Plancenoit and a further attempt was about to be made to storm this village.

The first assault on Plancenoit

Shortly before 6pm, the Prussian artillery on the crest facing Plancenoit opened up to prepare the assault on the village. Six of Hiller's battalions

The farm in Plancenoit. Just north of the church, this building stood in 1815, although many of the houses in the village were destroyed that day.

then closed in on their objective, advancing in battalion columns. Two more of Hiller's battalions moved through the Virère Wood on the north bank of the Lasne brook to cover his left flank. Hiller's remaining battalion had joined Losthin. Two of Losthin's battalions remained in action near to Fichermont. Hake and Ryssel moved up from the rear.

While Losthin engaged Lobau's men to the north of Plancenoit, Hiller stormed the village. Simmer's nine battalions defended their positions with great determination, but were forced back from the edge of the village into its centre. Here, the church with its high cemetery walls formed the strongpoint, looming up in front of the Prussian assault columns. A line of houses and hedges ran around the church, which today is in an open space. Simmer held on to these positions, despite French artillery pieces having been brought into the village and blasting the attackers with canister at point-blank range. The dead and wounded piled up on top of each other. Nevertheless, the Prussians pressed on, and by 6pm had all but captured the entire village. Their cannonballs now bounced in the direction of Napoleon's last reserve, the Imperial Guard.

The Emperor's attention was now distracted from Wellington's centre and he could not concentrate his efforts on the Duke without having dealt

View from the church to the south-east. A steep slope runs down this side of the church.

with this threat to his rear first. Eight battalions of the Young Guard under Duhesme were now sucked into this maelstrom, moving into Plancenoit about 6.45pm. They cleared the village rapidly, driving the Prussians back to the ravine to its east, where Ryssel was waiting to provide cover. The Young Guard deployed in defensive positions in the village and they would not now be able to join in the final attack on Wellington's centre. Napoleon's last blow against Wellington had been weakened, but the outcome of the battle was still in the balance.

Zieten's crucial decision

Meanwhile, Zieten had returned to his vanguard and he continued to move towards Wellington's left flank. He was perturbed by what he saw in front of him: Wellington's line was crumbling, masses of wounded and stragglers were moving to the rear, and Zieten suspected the collapse of Wellington's army was imminent. He halted his movement and sent an officer to inspect the situation at close quarters, who returned with the news that it looked like Wellington had lost the battle. The sight of Saxe-Weimar's Nassauers and Losthin's two battalions falling back from Smohain and Fichermont supported that view.

Fichermont. The Nassauers held on to this building all day until the Prussians came along and, mistaking them for French, finally drove them out of their positions.

As Zieten was considering what to do next, a staff officer arrived from Blücher. The Prussian high command had determined that the possession of Plancenoit would decide the battle, so all available troops were ordered to advance on it. Bülow was making little headway and the Young Guard was consolidating its hold on Plancenoit, so Zieten was instructed to move to his left and link up with Bülow. Just as Zieten was commencing this movement, Reiche returned from a conference with Saxe-Weimar. The situation on Wellington's left had deteriorated further and Reiche had assured Saxe-Weimar that help was about to arrive. Zieten decided that the order from headquarters must be obeyed. His men turned their backs on Wellington and started to move towards Plancenoit.

Müffling observed this and immediately galloped off towards Zieten. Words were exchanged and Müffling persuaded Zieten to change his mind and turn again, making for Wellington's left as quickly as possible. It was now nearly 7pm, and Ney had finally taken la Haye Sainte. Napoleon was again in control of Plancenoit and the Imperial Guard was preparing for the final assault on Wellington's centre. He had victory in his grasp.

Ney urging on his men. While the Prussians were attempting to seize Plancenoit, Ney finally took control of the farmhouse of la Haye Sainte, presenting the greatest threat to Wellington's centre that day.

PRINCE WILLEM FREDERIK CHARLES OF THE NETHERLANDS (1797-1881)

Born in exile in the Prussian Royal Palace in Berlin, Prince Frederik first saw action as an officer of the Prussian 2nd Foot Guards at the Battle of Grossgörschen (Lützen) in May 1813. That autumn, he fought with Zieten's Brigade in Kleist's Corps in the Army of Bohemia at the battles of Dresden, Kulm and Leipzig. He then returned to the Netherlands at the end of 1813 as part of the force under Bülow. Once Napoleon was expelled from his homeland, the Prince played a leading role in raising an army from his countrymen, which then fought against the French until Napoleon's first abdication. On Napoleon's return to France for the Hundred Days, he was placed in command of the II Corps of the Netherlands Army that held Hal until Waterloo. He then moved into France, commanding the forces besieging le Quesnoy and Valenciennes.

The second assault on Plancenoit

Hiller was now preparing to renew his attack on Plancenoit. Ryssel was moving up to support him. Once Ryssel had closed up, Hiller's battalions forced their way into Plancenoit a second time, along with two of Ryssel's. The French artillery again poured rounds of canister on the advancing Prussians at point blank range, while the Young Guard fired on them from behind the cover of the high wall around the churchyard. Two battalions of Pomeranian militia from Ryssel's brigade charged home, throwing back Napoleon's picked men, and the Pomeranians seized three French artillery pieces and took several hundred prisoners. However, the French continued to hold the houses around the church and fired on the Prussians from just thirty paces away.

The intensity of the fighting in the village grew. The Young Guard held on for as long as they could, but were eventually forced back. As more and more of them quit Plancenoit, Lobau was forced to pull back his men to avoid exposing his left flank. It was now around 7.15pm, and the Prussians were on the point of breaking through into Napoleon's rear. The only reserve he had left was the Old Guard. Just two battalions were ordered in to retrieve the situation and two battalions less were now available for the final assault on Wellington's centre, which again had to be delayed until Plancenoit was recovered.

Morand, the commander of the Chasseurs à Pied, ordered Pelet to take his first battalion to Plancenoit, where the Young Guard had been all but beaten. Pelet was aware of the serious situation. En route, he met Duhesme, the commander of the Young Guard, who was being held on his saddle after suffering a head wound from a musket ball. Two days later, Duhesme succumbed to this wound, dying in the inn of the Roi d'Espagne in Genappe, an event commemorated by a plaque there.

Moving closer to Plancenoit, Pelet then came across Chartrand, commander of the 1st Brigade of the Young Guard, who reported that the Prussians had captured the entire village. Hardly were the words out of his mouth when a broken battalion of Young Guardsmen came running their way, underlining the gravity of the situation. The mere sight of the Guard Chasseurs started to stabilise the situation, but the struggle was far from over. The lead platoon of the Chasseurs charged the advancing Prussians. The second platoon moved up in support. When the steam ran out of this counterattack, more companies were fed in. The fighting could hardly have been more vicious. The range was so close that there was little time left to reload

Memorial to Duhesme at Plancenoit. The commander of the Young Guard was mortally wounded in the fighting and was taken to the inn of the King of Spain in Genappe, where he later died.

fired muskets, so the Guardsmen had to make do with the bayonet and the butt. Just as the Chasseurs were starting to run out of momentum, the 1/2 Grenadiers à Pied arrived, their charge clearing the village at bayonet point.

The situation was now stabilised, at least long enough for the final assault against Wellington's centre to be launched. The Prussians had, however, not only irretrievably weakened Napoleon's last chance of breaking through Wellington's centre, but they had also bought the Duke enough time to shore up his crumbling line. Victory was slipping from Napoleon's grasp.

Plancenoit falls to the Prussians

Plancenoit remained in Napoleon's hands for only a short time. As the remainder of the Old Guard marched off for its final fateful encounter with Wellington's redcoats, more Prussians closed in on Plancenoit. As volleys of British musketry tossed Napoleon's Guardsmen into the air, Pirch I's Corps prepared to assault the village. As the first wave of Napoleon's final assault was thrown back, Tippelskirch's Brigade prepared to lead the attack that decided the battle. As the second wave of Guardsmen was enfiladed, then charged by Wellington's battalions, nine battalions of Prussians stormed Plancenoit. They advanced along three lines: one, consisting of three battalions, moved from the north, drawn inextricably towards the church; another, consisting of two battalions, approached this goal from the east. Three more battalions approached from the south. It was getting on for 8pm.

The church was ablaze and the houses were burning. The bitter house-to-house fighting continued, many of the wounded being consumed in the flames or slaughtered by their enemies. For a while, the Guard held its positions, but two battalions of Hiller's brigade were working their way up the Lasne defile, moving round the south of Plancenoit. Once they got into a position where they threatened the line of retreat from the village, the Guard had little option but to withdraw. This was done in good order, the Grenadiers falling back first and the Chasseurs covering their manoeuvre. There was no chance in the circumstances to recover their heavy equipment. The guns and ammunition waggons were left behind, the victor gaining the spoils of war. Wellington now ordered the general advance.

The Prussians broke out of Plancenoit and pushed on to the Brussels road. Order broke down on both sides, with the pursuers getting mixed up with the pursued. The two battalions of the Guard falling back from Plancenoit soon dissolved into the tide of retreat.

By 8.30pm, the battle had been decided. While most of the Army of the North degenerated into a fleeing mass, leaving behind much of its artillery, the Guard at least attempted to rally. Napoleon had kept back two battalions of the 1st Grenadiers at la Belle Alliance. Standing in squares, they tried to hold back the flood of broken men now running from the battlefield. Then they withdrew in good order, one across country, the other along the road to Namur, towards Rossomme. For a while, Napoleon took shelter in one of these squares, but the situation deteriorated so rapidly that he soon left them, riding with his staff back to le Caillou, where the 1/1 Chasseurs had been left. This battalion covered Napoleon's escape to Genappe.

55

A symbolic meeting of Wellington, Blücher and their men. But where did it really take place?

Napoleon's flight from Waterloo. When the pursuing Prussians closed in on Napoleon, he abandoned his coach, which was brimming with valuables, and rode hard to escape.

Much of the pursuit of the French stopped once they had quitted the field of battle. It was growing dark, the strenuous approach march had exhausted the Prussians and the day's battle had decimated Wellington's ranks. While a handful of Prussians continued towards Genappe, Wellington and Blücher met, some say at the inn of la Belle Alliance, a name with some symbolic value.

Weight of numbers eventually prevailed at Plancenoit and its fall decided the battle. Although it is difficult to be certain of the losses, the Prussians are likely to have suffered over 6,000 casualties in the struggle for this village, and the French at least 4,000. Most of these losses occurred in the street fighting in this normally peaceful village. The carnage and stench must have been horrific, with thousands of bodies packing the streets and burning in the houses. Significantly, Napoleon was forced to commit most of his infantry reserves to hold and then retake this vital position. Lobau was the first to face the Prussians, and when he could not hold his own, the entire Young Guard and later part of the Old Guard were committed. Napoleon was deprived of those very reserves he needed to win the battle. Thanks to the Prussians, Lobau was not available to take advantage of Wellington's deteriorating position and only part of Napoleon's last reserves could march against Wellington in the final attack of the day. Vivian's words echo here.

The meeting at la Belle Alliance

This building has seen several reincarnations since the battle and in recent years has served as a disco and then a Tex-Mex restaurant. The purist is no doubt horrified by such use of a historic monument, but the current use of this building is not the only point of contention, as accounts of the meeting vary, particularly regarding its location. Indeed, Wellington did not think it took place there at all. In a letter to the Waterloo historian William Mudford, dated 8 June 1816, Wellington complained about the many tall stories told about the battle. 'Of these,' he wrote, 'a remarkable instance is to be found in the report of a meeting between Marshal Blücher and me at La Belle Alliance; and some have gone so far as to have seen the chair on which I sat down in that farmhouse. It happens that the meeting took place after ten at night, at the village of Genappe.' Mudford's constant pestering of Wellington to gain official approval of his forthcoming book appears to have greatly annoyed the Duke, who would seem to have tried to divert his attention with a false trail. After all, Wellington's Waterloo Despatch mentioned how Blücher sent Wellington word on the morning of 19 June 1815 'that he had taken 60 pieces of cannon, belonging to the Imperial Guard and several carriages, baggage, etc. ... belonging to Bonaparte in

Genappe.' If Wellington had indeed met Blücher at Genappe at 10pm the previous evening, then he would have known that already. The story becomes more confusing, as the 5th Earl Stanford recorded a dinner conversation with Wellington on 4 November 1850, in which the Duke said, 'Blücher and I met near La Belle Alliance; we were both on horse back, but he embraced and kissed me, exclaiming "Mein Lieber Kamerad" and then "Quelle affaire!" which was pretty all he knew of French.'

As most accounts of this meeting record a discussion lasting ten to fifteen minutes, it is likely that a good deal more was said.

Wellington and Blücher meet at la Belle Alliance. In this version, Blücher takes his hat off to Wellington. That no doubt pleased the Duke.

Blücher and Wellington meeting at la Belle Alliance. This version shows a meeting of equals.

Müffling, as we know, was in close proximity to Wellington for much of the time. His memoirs mention the two commanders meeting towards the close of the battle and deciding that the Prussians should take over the pursuit of the French. Then, around midnight, when Müffling returned to Wellington's headquarters in Waterloo, he told the Duke that Blücher was intending to name the battle 'Belle Alliance'. Müffling's various histories of the campaign are inconsistent on this point, some claiming that this meeting took place near la Belle Alliance, others not mentioning its exact location. Several accounts of various participants, such as the then Lieutenant Basil Jackson of the Royal Staff Corps, who was later to join the staff of Sir Hudson Lowe, Napoleon's gaoler on St Helena, and Captain Gronow of the 1st Foot Guards, give la Belle Alliance as the location, but one cannot be certain of their accuracy.

One has to ask oneself the obvious question here. Why, when coming out of Plancenoit, would Blücher have turned north, towards Wellington, and not ridden south to direct his troops pursuing Napoleon? The route through Plancenoit that the Prussians took would have brought them onto the Brussels road somewhere between Rossomme and Maison-du-Roi.

Wellington's route would have taken him down the Brussels highway in a southerly direction. It is likely the two men met somewhere along this road. In this respect, the account of Constant Rebecque, the Prince of Orange's chief-of-staff, is most interesting. It reads:

> I rejoined the Duke [of Wellington], who was urging on the pursuit and we were attempting to move around the enemy's left flank on the highway beyond la Belle Alliance. Moving down the left of the highway, we saw the farm of Papelotte in flames, then the village of Plancenoit that the Prussians had taken.
>
> At Rossomme, we moved onto the highway and found it blocked with enemy cannon. Thanks to these guns, we had some trouble getting to the hamlet of la Maison du Roi. We then rode to the right into the fields and as it was ten o'clock in the evening, the Duke ordered the troops to halt and I carried this order to Colonel Detmer's Brigade that bivouacked between la Maison du Roi and the Caillou [Chantelet] Wood.
>
> We accompanied the Duke back to the highway, rejoining it between the farm of le Caillou and la Maison du Roi. It was here that we

The farmhouse of le Caillou. This is where Napoleon set up his headquarters on the night before Waterloo. Was it nearer here that Wellington and Blücher had their legendary meeting?

Röchling's painting shows Pomeranian infantry seeing off the Old Guard towards the end of the day's struggle for possession of Plancenoit.

Northen's famous painting of the Prussians storming the village of Plancenoit gives a very good impression of the terrifying nature of this battle.

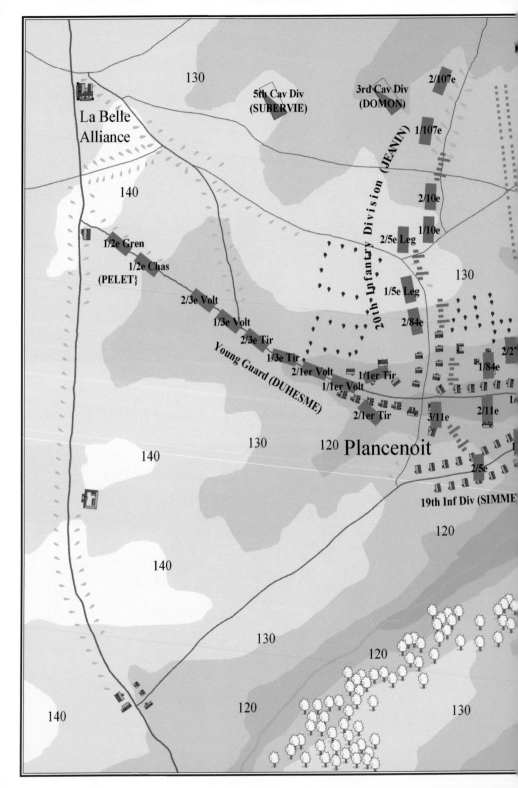

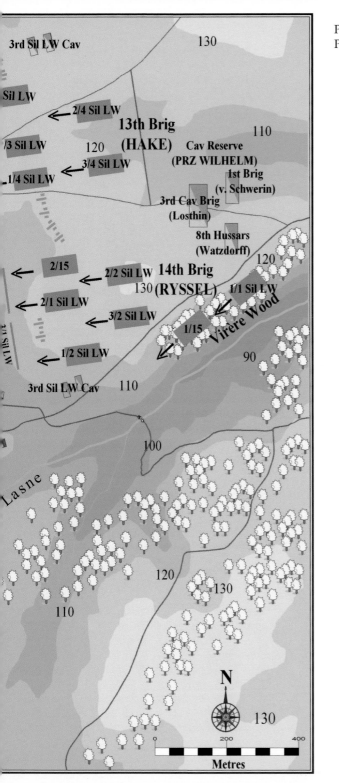

Plancenoit, the second
Prussian assault, 6-7.30pm.

Prussian line infantry engage Napoleon's Old Guard at Plancenoit. This painting by Baux captures the close-quarter fighting for the village.

Napoleon's isolation during his voyage to exile on the Atlantic island of St Helena was more than merely symbolic. The era that bears his name came to an end.

encountered Field-Marshal Blücher, General von Bülow and their staff.

We greeted each other and agreed that the Prussians should continue the pursuit.

It is also interesting to note that towards the close of the battle, Wellington requested Bülow to cease firing his artillery in the direction of la Belle Alliance as the Duke was about to storm it. That would indicate that Wellington's men took this position and not the Prussians. The Prussian artillery was firing from the direction of Plancenoit, to the southeast, which places their commanders in or near that village. As the French then retreated southwards, the attention of the Prussian high command is likely to have followed them.

Most early accounts of the campaign give la Belle Alliance as the place the two commanders met and had a conversation lasting ten to fifteen minutes, but it may well have been further along the Brussels highway that this conference took place. All that is certain is that it was not in Genappe.

The inn of la Belle Alliance as it is today. Take care when crossing this busy road!

The plaque to the French Medical Corps on the wall of la Belle Alliance.

Blücher's decision to name the battle after la Belle Alliance appears to have been an afterthought and does not necessarily indicate that the meeting took place there. Nevertheless, there is a plaque on the wall of the inn of la Belle Alliance commemorating this meeting and there are many paintings of it.

The pursuit

Although the Imperial Guard retired from Plancenoit in good order, it was not long before it too fell apart and joined the chaotic flight from the battlefield, this happening before it reached le Caillou. Some artillery tried to cover the retreat, but only enough gunners to man one piece held their ground, and even then not long enough to achieve anything. Pursuing Prussian cavalry forced the Guard into square, delaying its withdrawal. For a while, these squares maintained order and withdrew in a chequerboard formation, holding off the cavalry. A battalon of Prussian infantry moved through the Chantelet Wood, threatening the flank of the retiring French. The withdrawal was accelerated, but once the squares reached the Brussels highway, all order broke down and Napoleon's élite joined the fleeing masses. There was now no longer a rearguard left to cover the retreat.

With the road to Charleroi now open, the Prussians started their pursuit. General von Roeder, the commander of Zieten's cavalry, led two of his regiment to Genappe, where he came across Gneisenau, who was at the head of 400 Prussian fusiliers. They had already captured seventy-eight French cannon, assorted limbers and waggons, 2,000 men and several generals. Nevertheless, some of the retreating French attempted to make a stand here, blocking the narrow entrance to the village with guns and waggons, setting light to some of the buildings and firing on the Prussians. Napoleon was still in Genappe and was now forced to abandon his carriage in such a rush that he left behind his sword and dropped his hat. These were some of the smaller trophies the Prussians took that day. Panic then broke out in Genappe and the attempt to defend it ceased. Some of Roeder's troopers dismounted and cleared the entrance to the village, doing so without molestation. In the moonlight, they saw six carriages at the end of the high street, which were to be one of the richer prizes of that day.

Napoleon rode off towards Charleroi and into the night, leaving behind his personal baggage train. The horses were still harnessed to each of the six carriages, but there was not a Frenchman in sight. Zieten's troopers helped themselves to handfuls of booty as they rode past, but left most of the contents to the following fusiliers. Their commanding officer took charge of Napoleon's medals and a set of diamonds said to be worth a million francs. Some of these precious stones were presented to the King of Prussia and were later mounted in the crown jewels, but part of this booty is reported to have disappeared.

The pursuing Prussians caught up with Napoleon's treasury waggon, headquarters baggage and his marshals' personal waggons at les Bons Villers, just north of Charleroi. The treasury waggon contained thousands of gold coins and this was the last major prize of the day.

It is interesting to note that while much of the French artillery was lost and many valuables taken, not a single eagle fell into Allied hands during this pursuit. This indicates that the infantry maintained some sort of order. The pursuit petered out in the dark and was broken off somewhere along the Charleroi road.

Chapter Six

The Battle of Wavre, 18/19 June 1815

Grouchy's positions and movements

We discussed the general area of Wavre earlier, during the description of the Prussian withdrawal from the field of Ligny. Grouchy moved up through the same terrain. We also examined the terrain north and west of Wavre when outlining the Prussian movement to Plancenoit. We left Grouchy at 10pm on the evening of 17 June 1815, closing up on the Prussians in and around Wavre. Vandamme and Gérard's Corps arrived in Gembloux late that evening. Teste's Division from Reille's Corps bivouacked at Mazy, south of Gembloux, along with Soult's Cavalry Division. Exelmans' dragoons spent the night at Sauvenière, north-east of Gembloux, up the road to Tienen. Grouchy's men were soaked from that day's torrential rain and covered with the mud they had waded through from Ligny. This night was uncomfortable for all the participants.

Pajol's cavalry patrols covered the area from Mazy to Temploux, in the direction of Namur, where they found no sign of the Prussians. His patrols then moved north, to Leez, to attempt to find any Prussians in that area. While Pajol was conducting this search, reports came in to Grouchy's headquarters that the Prussians had abandoned Tourinnes, to the north of Gembloux. At 3am on 18 June, Grouchy ordered Pajol to continue his movement from Leez to Tourinnes. Shortly after that, a report arrived of the sighting of a Prussian artillery park at Leez, which Pajol was then ordered to capture.

At 6am, Grouchy reported to Napoleon that the Prussians appeared to be falling back in the direction of Brussels. He thought it likely that they were either going to concentrate there, or move to join Wellington. He informed Napoleon that there were no Prussians in the area of Namur. Furthermore, he reported that Zieten was moving on Corbais, and Pirch I towards Chaumont, having marched through the night. Grouchy also indicated it was his intention to start immediately for Wavre, marching though Sart-à-Walhain and Corbais, and he would keep Napoleon informed of any developments. This message is likely to have reached Napoleon by 10am, so the Battle of Waterloo started with him knowing that he was likely to have to face the Prussians as well that day.

Reference to any of the cartography available in Napoleon's headquarters would have indicated how unlikely it was for Grouchy, in his

MARSHAL COUNT EMMANUEL DE GROUCHY (1766–1847)

A soldier of the royal army, Grouchy trained at the artillery school in Strasbourg, receiving his commission in 1781. Three years later, he transferred to the cavalry, and from there to the royal guard in 1786. During the Revolutionary Wars, he came to command his own cavalry regiment and helped to put down the royalist uprisings in the Vendée. Made a general in 1795, the next year he participated in the ill-fated expedition to Ireland. He was in the thick of it in Italy in 1799, fighting at Novi in August, and received fourteen wounds in that campaign. In 1800, he commanded a division under Moreau at Hohenlinden. The next year, he was made inspector-general of the cavalry. In 1804, he commanded a division during the occupation of the Netherlands. The next year, he fought at Ulm and, in the Jena campaign of 1806, commanded a cavalry division under Murat. In 1807, he was wounded at Eylau and fought again at Friedland. He was sent to Spain in 1808, spending a short time as governor of Madrid. In 1809 he commanded a division of dragoons in the Army of Italy under Eugène de Beauharnais, fighting in the siege of Graz and finally at Wagram. Wounded at Borodino in 1812, he fought in the retreat from Moscow, but was so ill for much of 1813 that he saw little active service. Returning to the ranks in 1814, he fought in the defence of France. In March 1815 he joined Napoleon, defeating a royalist army. He was the last person Napoleon made a Marshal of the Empire. Placed in command of the cavalry in 1815, he conducted the pursuit of the Prussians after Ligny. Blamed by some for not having marched to the sound of the guns on 18 June, an impossible feat to accomplish in the circumstances, he restored order in the army after Waterloo and conducted an exemplary retreat to Paris. Exiled to Philadelphia, he returned to France in 1820.

current positions, to be able to intercept the Prussian movement. The defile of the Dyle river, flooded by the previous day's torrential rain, would be impassable save only at a few points where there were bridges. The Prussians were likely to be holding these places and even a few men could delay any attempt by Grouchy to cut through the line of Prussian columns marching to Waterloo. Not only was it clear to Napoleon that he had to expect to fight the Prussians later that day, but he would also have to do so without Grouchy. He accepted battle with Wellington on that basis.

At 10am, Grouchy, now in Sart-à-Walhain, sent a further report to Napoleon, giving him more up-to-date information. He reported that three Prussian army corps were apparently marching in the direction of Brussels, two of which had passed through Sart-à-Walhain the previous day. He also identified that a fourth corps (Bülow) had joined the others, having moved from Liège. Grouchy also mentioned that the Prussian officers had talked about moving to link up with Wellington. Finally, Grouchy indicated he expected to be massed in front of Wavre by the coming evening. Napoleon is likely to have received this report by 2pm. He continued the battle in the knowledge that the Prussians were intending to join Wellington and that Grouchy could do nothing to stop them.

From around 11.30am, Grouchy could hear the cannon fire coming from Waterloo. Gérard suggested they march towards the sounds of battle, but Grouchy declined, pointing out that his orders were to pursue the Prussians. His decision is much criticised, but let us not forget that the Prussians required eleven hours to cover the shorter distance from Dion-le-Mont to Plancenoit, the delays being caused largely by the muddy terrain. Had any of the choke points on this route been blocked, then they might never have arrived at all. Had Grouchy moved on Waterloo immediately, Napoleon would have been in Charleroi, minus his baggage, sword, hat, gold and diamonds, before Grouchy could have reached the battlefield, assuming, of course, that the Prussians made no efforts to hold him up. Napoleon's delay in issuing orders for the pursuit on the morning of 16 June was in part to blame for the trail growing cold. The 8,000 Prussians that ran for Namur misled the French sufficiently to make it impossible for Grouchy to prevent Blücher from joining Wellington.

News then came in that Exelmans' patrols had located a strong Prussian rearguard in the woods on the heights immediately south of Wavre. This confirmed that the Prussians had crossed the Dyle and were on their way to join Wellington. They had a seven-hour start over Grouchy and had blocked the main crossing point over the swollen Dyle. All that Grouchy could now do to assist Napoleon was to engage as many Prussians as he could, reducing the number they could send to Waterloo, which is

PRINCE FRIEDRICH WILHELM HEINRICH AUGUST OF PRUSSIA (1779–1843)

Known as Prince August, he joined the Infantry Regiment Alt-Larisch (No.26) as a captain in 1797, aged eighteen. Having missed the Revolutionary Wars, he first saw action at Jena in 1806 as a lieutenant-colonel commanding the grenadier battalion of the Infantry Regiment von Arnim (No.13). He received a commendation for his role in the campaign, and was released from captivity in France at the end of 1807. In 1808, he was appointed inspector-general of the entire Prussian artillery, as well as being colonel-in-chief of the East Prussian Artillery Regiment. The Prince then played an active role in the campaigns of 1813–15, fighting in several crucial battles, winning the Iron Cross at Grossgörschen (Lützen) in May 1813, before being given command of a brigade in the II Army Corps that autumn. His role in rallying his troops at the Battle of Kulm on 30 August 1813 deserves particular mention. Promoted to full general at the end of the campaign of 1814, he was given command of the II Army Corps on 30 June 1815, and led the siege operations in northern France until the end of the war. In 1830, the Prince was appointed inspector-general of the Prussian artillery.

precisely what he did. Had it not been for Grouchy, then the whole Prussian army would have arrived at Waterloo, overwhelming Napoleon earlier in the day.

The situation on the morning of 18 June

Wavre was situated on the Dyle river, which, thanks to the recent heavy rain, was not fordable. The meadows lining the riverside were marshy and in places flooded, so the few bridges over it became the focal points of the battle for the possession of this town. Two stone bridges stood in Wavre itself, the Namur to Brussels highway running over one of these. There were wooden bridges to the south-west at Limelette, Limal and near the mill of Bierges, and to the north-east at Bas-Wavre. On the northern – that is Prussian – side of the Dyle at Wavre, the ground rose steeply up towards the Château de la Bawette.

Thielemann's corps had spent the night of 17/18 June bivouacked around la Bawette. Early on the morning of 18 June, he had received orders to form the rearguard and then follow the remainder of the Prussian army to Waterloo. Borcke's Brigade was ordered to cover this movement by holding Wavre. Two of his battalions took up positions around the large stone bridge, now the Pont du Christ, as well as in the suburb of the town south of the Dyle. Borcke mistook the I Army Corps for his own, and when they marched off towards St Lambert and Ohain, the remainder of his brigade followed in its footsteps. Thielemann lost touch with these troops.

During the afternoon of 18 June, strong French forces drew up on the southern bank of the Dyle, so Thielemann deployed the remainder of his men to cover this threat to Blücher's rear. Kemphen drew up on the heights to the north-west of Wavre, Luck to the north along the Brussels highway, while Stülpnagel covered the bridge at Bierges. The Reserve Cavalry was positioned to the rear of Kemphen's Brigade. In all, Thielemann had around 15,000 men available, including parts of Zieten's Corps.

Grouchy had double that number at his disposal, though only around half of his men were committed to that day's battle. Vandamme's Corps approached Wavre during the afternoon of 18 June. From the heights south of Wavre, it was evident to Vandamme that possession of the two bridges in Wavre was essential, so ignoring his orders to halt here, he sent his men down into the valley to attempt to seize the bridges. The battle commenced at 4pm, just before Bülow's Prussians engaged Lobau at Plancenoit, with two, then a third French battery opening up on the Prussians, before Vandamme ordered Habert's Division to assault the bridges.

The battle for Wavre, 18 June

Grouchy now arrived with Soult's orders of 10am to take Wavre. He decided to extend the attacks on Wavre to above and below the town and to attempt to seize several bridges. Exelmans was sent to Bas-Wavre, along with a battalion of infantry, and Lefol's Division of Vandamme's Corps moved on Bierges. Pajol's cavalry and Teste's Division were directed to move towards Limal and St Lambert to keep in contact with Napoleon.

Two companies of Prussian militia held Bas-Wavre, Berliners from the fusilier battalion of the 1st Kurmarkers under Major von Bornstedt. Hardly had they started to destroy the wooden bridge there when the French attack started. Under artillery fire, the Prussians removed some timbers, but had to stop when French skirmishers approached. The struggle for possession of the bridge continued for several hours without any decision.

Two more of Bornstedt's companies held the stone bridge in Wavre. For a while, the Prussian skirmishers in the southern suburb of Wavre held off the French assaults, but eventually the weight of numbers told and the Prussian defence collapsed. Seizing the advantage, the French moved rapidly across the stone bridge and the battle for Wavre commenced.

Heavy street fighting broke out, with the Prussians feeding in reinforcements from Luck's Brigade to stabilise the situation. After vicious fighting at close quarters in which no quarter was given, Habert's Division was thrown back across the Dyle and the General himself was wounded.

Now it was the turn of the French to stage a counterattack. Fresh troops regained the stone bridge and moved on into the centre of Wavre, pushing down the main road. Two battalions of Prussians were ready in the side streets and fired at point-blank range into the flanks of the advancing French. The attack was halted and a bayonet charge forced the French back over the bridge.

The fight for Bas-Wavre continued. The Prussians fed in more troops to stabilise the situation and managed to hold on to the bridge, although the French managed to capture a few houses.

GENERAL MAURICE-ÉTIENNE COUNT GÉRARD (1773-1852)

Gérard volunteered for an infantry battalion in the Revolutionary Wars and rose through the ranks, fighting at Neerwinden in 1793, Fleurus in 1794 and in many other actions, including in Italy in 1796. As an ADC of Bernadotte, he was wounded at Austerlitz in December 1805. In 1806, he fought at Halle and Lübeck before being promoted to general. In 1807, he commanded a brigade at Eylau. In 1809, he served as chief-of-staff of Bernadotte's Saxon Corps, fighting at Wagram, where he commanded the Saxon cavalry. The next year, he was sent to Spain, remaining there until he was transferred to Russia in 1812. Here, he commanded an infantry division and fought as part of the rearguard during the retreat from Moscow. In the spring of 1813, he commanded a division at Lützen and Bautzen and that autumn he received his own corps. He was wounded at the Battle on the Katzbach on 26 August, and again at Leipzig that October. Recovering from his wounds that winter, he fought at Brienne and la Rothière and in other actions. He had little problem finding service under the restored Bourbons and quickly rejoined Napoleon in 1815. He fought in the battle for Charleroi on 15 June, Ligny on 16 June and was wounded at Wavre on 18 June. After Napoleon's second abdication, he spent two years residing in the Netherlands before returning to Paris in 1817. He then spent several years in politics before being reappointed to the army in 1830, seeing action in Belgium in 1832.

Church of Jean le Baptiste in Wavre. There are memorials inside worth seeing.

The mill of Bierges stood out like a rocky island in the flooded and boggy ground around it. Close to it was the bridge that Lefol wanted to cross. One company of Prussian infantry held the mill, with infantry and artillery to the rear, in support. Hulot's Division of Gérard's Corps closed in on the Prussian positions with Gérard at its head. He was shot and severely wounded and the attack was repelled.

Around 6 to 7pm, Grouchy received Soult's orders of 1pm instructing him to move to join Napoleon. Grouchy then ordered Pajol to press on Limal and went to la Baraque, where he hoped to be able to lead the remaining divisions of Gérard's Corps to Limal. As they were not there, he sent them orders for this movement and returned to Wavre, where these divisions, having lost their way, arrived shortly afterwards. Grouchy then led them to Limal, arriving there at 11pm. Pajol was in control of the village, having seized the bridge earlier. Here, Gérard's Corps crossed the Dyle and clashed with Prussian troops from Stülpnagel's Brigade moving on Limal, driving them back in the dark. The pickets fired at each other for much of the night.

Having gained a bridgehead, Grouchy sent for Vandamme, instructing him to cross the Dyle at Limal, leaving just enough men to hold the bridges in Wavre. That night, rumours about the fighting at Waterloo spread through the bivouacked troops on both sides. Grouchy heard that Napoleon had been victorious, while Thielemann was told of a French defeat.

The situation on the morning of 19 June

Despite his orders, Vandamme sent only some of his men to join Grouchy, Hulot's Division and Exelmans' cavalry, leaving the rest in Wavre. The presence of such a large body of French soldiers tied down the Prussian defenders there.

Meanwhile, Stülpnagel deployed six of his battalions along the southern edge of the Rixensart Wood, and three more at the Point du Jour. From there to Bierges, five of Kemphen's battalions formed up with cavalry support. The rest of Kemphen's battalions held their positions along the Dyle near the mill of Bierges. A battle-group of seven battalions from

GENERAL DOMINIQUE-JOSEPH-RENÉ VANDAMME, COUNT D'UNSEBOURG (1770–1830)

Vandamme's military career began in 1788 as a private soldier in a French colonial regiment in the West Indies. Returning to France two years later, he joined an infantry regiment and was later commissioned. He first fought in the Revolutionary Wars as an officer in a free corps and rose through the ranks rapidly, fighting numerous actions. He attained the rank of general in February 1799. His role in the storming of the Pratzen Heights in the Battle of Austerlitz in December 1805 brought him a substantial financial reward. In 1806/7, he served in various sieges of fortresses in Prussia and was made second-in-command in Jérôme Bonaparte's Corps. In 1809, he led the Württemberg Corps in the Grande Armée, fighting at Abensberg, Landshut and Eckmühl before taking over command of the VII Corps and participating in the decisive Battle of Wagram. He also commanded a corps in the Russian campaign of 1812, but his excessive plundering led to him being sent home. In the spring of 1813, he commanded a corps under Davoût on the Lower Elbe around Hamburg. That autumn, his corps was wiped out at Kulm on 30 August when pursuing the defeated Allies after the Battle of Dresden and Vandamme was taken prisoner. Released after Napoleon's first abdication in 1814, he did not find favour with the restored Bourbons, but Napoleon reinstated him in 1815. In the Waterloo campaign he fought at Ligny and Wavre before being wounded at Namur. He commanded the rearguard during the retreat to Paris. He was then exiled from France until 1819.

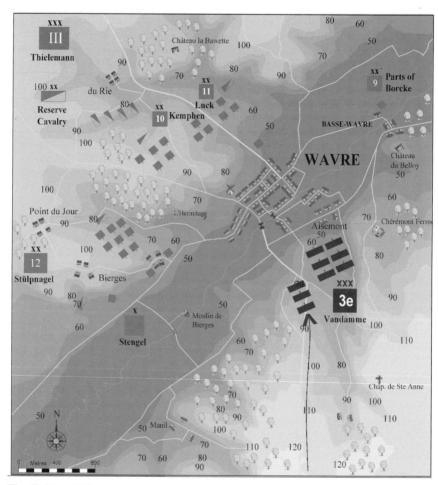

The Battle of Wavre

various brigades held Wavre, with cavalry and a regiment of militia in reserve to the rear. The remnant of Zieten's Corps, which had been at Wavre on 18 June, on hearing news of the victory over Napoleon, left to rejoin their corps.

Grouchy had four divisions of infantry available, along with the cavalry of Pajol and Exelmans. The French here enjoyed both the superiority in numbers, double that of the Prussians, as well as a larger number of cannon. Thielemann's position was precarious.

The Battle of Wavre, 19 June

The day's fighting commenced with an artillery duel in which the superior French artillery prevailed. After the Prussians had five guns damaged, Grouchy ordered three divisions and supporting cavalry to attack the Prussian positions. Stülpnagel fell back, but Kemphen held on to Bierges. Grouchy was forcing Thielemann away to the east, opening the road to Waterloo. He was clearly intending to join Napoleon. However, once confirmed news of the Allied victory arrived, the Prussians staged a counterattack, expecting the French to fall back. To their surprise, French reinforcements were committed and the Prussians driven back again.

Isolated and outnumbered, Thielemann decided the best course of action was to withdraw. He was forced to abandon five cannon.

Having brushed off Thielemann, Grouchy turned to march on Brussels, but at 10.30am the news of Napoleon's retreat arrived. Not having full details, Grouchy considered it too risky to continue his march and instead, after consulting his senior officers, decided to withdraw to Namur. Exelmans was instructed to gain and hold the bridges across the Sambre, while Gérard's Corps was sent via Limal and Gembloux to the Nivelles to Namur highway. The French disengaged during the night and the next morning the Prussians woke to find them gone. Grouchy's skilful withdrawal preserved his wing of the Army of the North, and gave Napoleon's wing a rallying point and a chance of rejoining battle. Thanks to Grouchy, the war was far from over.

Chapter Seven

The Aftermath

The situation on the night of 18/19 June 1815

For many, the end of the Battle of Waterloo on 18 June 1815 marks the end of the campaign that shares the same name. However, that was not the reality of the situation on the night of 18/19 June. Both Wellington's and Blücher's armies were exhausted and not able to carry out an effective pursuit of Napoleon's broken force. Thielemann's Corps was out on a limb, while Grouchy's wing of the Army of the North was intact and ready to join battle at any time. Furthermore, Napoleon was still at large and capable of bringing new forces into action. There was nothing to stop Napoleon rallying his men on Grouchy, bringing up fresh forces from Paris and staging a further offensive. Indeed, Napoleon had shown himself well capable of recovering rapidly from such set-backs in the 1814 campaign in France, and there was every reason to expect him to do the same after Waterloo. A battle had been won, but the campaign was far from over. To be won, the war had to be taken to Paris, and between Waterloo and Paris stood a formidable line of fortresses protecting northern France, commanded by men loyal to Bonaparte.

Wellington's army bivouacked that night on the field of victory, trying to sleep among the moans of the wounded. Much of the Prussian army had reached the battlefield during the course of 18 June, and more came up that night. While Wellington returned to Brussels to finish writing his Waterloo Despatch, Gneisenau spent the morning drafting orders for the advance into France. It was the Prussian army that did the most to see that the victory at Waterloo was transformed into Napoleon's final defeat.

The pursuit into France

The first potential bottleneck that Napoleon could use to delay the advance into France would be at the crossing of the Sambre river. Zieten was ordered to march as far as Charleroi that day, taking the bridges there. Pirch I was ordered to Anderlues to cut off Grouchy's line of retreat, receiving his orders before Grouchy had news of Napoleon's defeat. Bülow was sent to Fontaine l'Evêque to establish a line of communication with Mons and arrange for supplies to be sent on. The Prussians marched for most of the day, stopping only that evening. Wellington's army only moved as far as Nivelles. The Prussians were taking the lead and were determined to be the first in Paris.

By the evening of 19 June, Zieten had reached Charleroi and secured the bridges. Bülow bivouacked in the area of Fontaine l'Evêque and Souvret. Elements of Pirch I's Corps had reached Anderlues and Thielemann was in St-Agatha-Rode and Limal.

Grouchy's wing of the army had broken off contact with the Prussians. Gérard spent the night of 19/20 June in the area of le Boquet, Vandamme around la Falize, Pajol at Gembloux and Exelmans in Namur.

Napoleon's wing was beginning to recover from its defeat. Parts of d'Erlon's and Reille's Corps rallied in Beaumont and Philippeville, and were brought back to Avesnes. Together with men from Jérôme's Division, a fighting force of 12,000 men was assembled. More men arrived in Avesnes, including several thousands from the Imperial Guard, Lobau's Corps and the reserve cavalry used at Waterloo. The Prussians had lost contact with this wing of the French army as well.

The information coming into Blücher's headquarters was confused. Contact with Thielemann had been lost, but there were reports of a battle with Grouchy at Wavre. Patrols were sent out on 20 June to establish the whereabouts of the French forces, troops were sent to Maubeuge to seize the crossings over the Sambre there and Wellington was sent a request for ammunition, particularly for the howitzer and mortar rounds soon to be used against the French fortresses. The stage was now set to take the war into France.

Wellington and Blücher had different objectives. Wellington merely wanted to restore the status quo *ante bellum*, while Blücher wanted to extract revenge and plunder from France. While Wellington gathered his forces and pondered what he should do next, Blücher plunged headlong across the border, intending to force march his already exhausted and ill-supplied men all the way to Paris. If the Prussians got there first, then Blücher would be in a better position to enforce his claims. Wellington instructed his army to respect the French and pay for all their requisitions, but Blücher's memories of the French occupation of Prussia had not faded. He was going to blaze a trail all the way to Paris, sending home all the booty he could lay his hands on. As the Prussians were about to commence the investment of the French fortress of Maubeuge, Wellington's men had not even regained the positions they had at the start of the campaign. The race to Paris started with Blücher having his nose ahead.

The race to Paris

After such a dramatic victory, Blücher was elated and determined to move on Paris as fast as he could. However, his army's supply system had already broken down during the advance to Waterloo and that June was

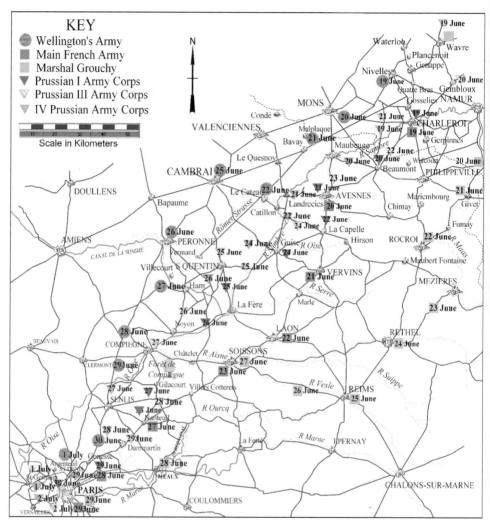

The Race to Paris

hot indeed, so Gneisenau endeavoured to moderate Blücher's objectives. He did not, however, obtain the much-needed day of rest for his men.

Napoleon was very much aware of what the next objective of the Prussians would be. From Philippeville, where he spent the night of 18/19

June, he sent orders to Alsace and the Vendée for his men there to move on the capital.

On the morning of 20 June, Blücher considered it likely that Grouchy had reached Namur and, as such, it would now be impossible to stop him crossing the Meuse River. That being the case, Blücher directed part of his army, including the Corps of Zieten, Bülow and part of Pirch I's, to Avesnes, on the highway to Paris.

Other elements from Pirch I's Corps were sent to establish contact with Thielemann and Grouchy's withdrawing columns clashed with them that day as Grouchy fell back on Namur. That morning Grouchy staged a fighting withdrawal, then in the afternoon retired into the city through the Brussels gate with Pirch I's vanguard hard on his heels. Strong French

Avesnes. Fortunately, many of the fortifications here have survived and they are well worth a visit.

The site of the Powder Magazine at Avesnes.

forces then held this position, driving back the Prussians in a battle that continued until early evening. Between 6 and 8pm, Grouchy pulled out of Namur and marched on Dinant. The Prussians did not pursue him as piles of burning wood left behind on the bridges held them up.

On 21 June, Zieten was ordered to blockade the fortress of Avesnes, while Bülow was directed towards Maubeuge, as was most of Pirch I's Corps. The same day orders were sent to the North German Federal Army to link up with the left wing of his forces and then march for Sedan.

Zieten's vanguard reached Avesnes at 4pm that day. All the howitzers of his corps' reserve artillery were brought up and once Zieten's demand for capitulation was rejected, the bombardment of this fortress began. Avesnes had been an important base for Napoleon's Armée du Nord, and unless this strongly built Vauban fortress fell into Prussian hands quickly, it would remain a considerable obstruction to the advance on Paris. At 8pm the bombardment stopped for a while and a sortie by the garrison was thrown back. As the French were staging a determined defence, Zieten considered leaving some of his men to blockade the fortress, while continuing to march on Paris with the rest.

At midnight, at the request of Colonel Lehmann, commander of the reserve artillery, the Prussian howitzers opened up again. Zieten did not think this would have much effect, but the fourteenth round struck lucky, hitting the powder magazine, blowing it up and lighting up the night sky. The garrison of just over 200 men capitulated the next morning and the Prussians captured substantial supplies, including 47 heavy guns with 15,000 rounds of ammunition and a million musket cartridges. Zieten could now continue to Paris with a supply depot to his rear instead of the hostile base of operations he was expecting.

Bülow reached Maubeuge early on 21 June. The fortress commandant there refused to surrender, so Bülow brought up the remainder of his corps and commenced a blockade of the fortress.

Blücher's men had already crossed the French border before Wellington entered French territory. The Duke did so on 21 June, moving to Bavay and investing both Valenciennes and le Quesnoy. That afternoon, Blücher decided to march for Paris with three of his corps, and left one to deal with the various fortresses in northern France. Wellington was already lagging behind. When pressed on this by Müffling, Wellington explained that he was not prepared to leave his supply trains behind and rush headlong into France.

Grouchy continued his withdrawal, passing Dinant that day with both Thielemann and Pirch I on his trail. He reached Givet, where his men enjoyed their first freshly baked bread for three days. As this fort's stocks of ammunition were insufficient, Grouchy was not able to resupply his men. Napoleon had yet to send him any orders, so Grouchy decided to try to establish contact via Laon.

The remnants of d'Erlon's and Reille's Corps reached Vervins on 21 June.

At noon on 22 June, Zieten departed from Avesnes, leaving two battalions behind to garrison it. Bülow left a small force blockading Landrecies, while the remainder of his force continued towards Paris.

Two of Pirch I's brigades were ordered to invest Maubeuge, while sending off detachments to observe and blockade other fortresses, relieving any other forces undertaking such activities. Elements of this corps then moved on to Landrecies, Chimay, Mariembourg, Philippeville and Givet-Charlemont, intending to link up with Kleist's North Germans.

Part of Wellington's army continued its march into France that day, but it was already one day behind Blücher. The race to Paris had hardly begun, but the Prussians already had a significant lead.

Napoleon abdicated in favour of his son and a provisional government was formed in Paris that tended towards Louis XVIII. The king now crossed the border into France along with his royal guard, and the local population welcomed him.

Grouchy, however, remained in the field, sending his IV Corps, now commanded by General Vichery, to Rocroi. Vandamme objected to the entire army being forced down one road and had the western flank covered by cavalry. Detachments were sent to Philippeville, Mariembourg, Chimay and Hirson. Reports came in of Prussian movements at Thuin, Gerpinnes and Walcourt. Orders arrived from Napoleon instructing him to move via Rheims to Soissons.

D'Erlon and Reille reached Laon, where troops that Soult had sent from Philippeville joined them. The remnants of Lobau's Corps were divided between d'Erlon and Reille. Elements of the Imperial Guard and the reserve cavalry also gathered here.

Soult now had 20–25,000 men available, but one-third did not have arms, and there was very little artillery to hand. The infantry was resupplied from the stocks in Laon and Soissons and great efforts were made to restore military discipline to these broken troops. The army was demoralised, with the men deserting in large numbers, and the local farmers were refusing to hand over supplies. Soult wrote to Napoleon in Paris to inform him of the situation, and to say that he was withdrawing rather than fighting.

On 23 June, Zieten and Bülow were finally allowed a welcome day of rest, allowing Thielemann to catch up with them. Thielemann took the opportunity to resupply his men from the vast stocks captured at Avesnes. Elements of Pirch I's Corps garrisoned Avesnes, while more Prussian troops were ordered up from the Rhine to relieve them.

A French emissary delivered a note to Blücher informing him of Napoleon's abdication. He pointed out that the Allies had declared war on Napoleon, not France, and with Napoleon gone, a state of peace had surely returned, but Blücher rejected these overtures. He would not be put off gaining revenge and extracting plunder so easily.

Prince August of Prussia was now placed in command of the II Army Corps and the North German Federal Army Corps and he was ordered to take overall charge of the sieges.

The same day, reports came in of French troops gathering in Laon under the command of Marshal Soult. Troop movements from Lorraine into the interior were also reported. It seemed as if a new army was being assembled to defend Paris.

Wellington went to Blücher's headquarters that day to try to come to an agreement with Blücher on the further conduct of the war. It seemed that the Duke had now realised that the Prussians were making for Paris at full speed and perceived the dangers this entailed. Both parties to this discussion agreed on a joint march to the capital of France, but as Wellington's supply trains were slow in coming up, Blücher soon forged ahead again, now moving on the Oise river.

While three Prussian army corps were marching directly on Paris, various cavalry detachments were sent deep into French territory as raiding parties, patrols and to seize important points. They clashed with the French on numerous occasions.

Ignoring his orders, Grouchy sent Vandamme off towards Laon and his artillery to Mézières, where it could be resupplied with ammunition. Vichery was sent via Rocroi to Maubert-Fontaine, acting as a vanguard. His cavalry covered the western flank. Reports came in of Prussian strong forces in la Capelle, and patrols in Hirson, Vervins and Marle, supporting the contention that they were moving on Laon. Grouchy decided to move eastwards. Soult began to withdraw his men down the highway to Soissons.

The Provisional Government attempted to negotiate a ceasefire with Blücher. He repeated his terms: the handing over of Napoleon, the surrender of Paris and all fortresses on the Moselle, Meuse and Sambre. These demands were not accepted, so the war continued.

On the night of 23/24 June, elements of Bülow's Corps bombarded the fort of Guise. Next morning, Zieten relieved him and issued a further demand to the fort's commandant for surrender. It was rejected, so Zieten brought up a howitzer battery. The mere threat of using it was sufficient to induce the commandant to capitulate and further supplies fell into Prussian hands.

Reports came in that morning of 30–40,000 French troops moving from Laon to Soissons. The same day, Wellington opened fire on the fortress of Cambrai, the walls of which were in poor condition. A small fire started in the town and that evening men of Colville's 4th Division stormed the fortress. While the redcoats scaled the walls, Royalist sympathisers fought with the garrison. The town and its walls were now in Allied hands, but the commandant withdrew into the citadel, finally capitulating on 25 June on the understanding that the fortress was handed over to Louis XVIII.

Grouchy sent Vichery to Rethel and ordered Vandamme to close on him. Vandamme did not carry out his orders in full. On arriving in Rethel, Grouchy received news of Napoleon's abdication and a message from Marshal Davoût, the minister of war, instructing him to move on Paris. Grouchy informed Davoût that he was directing all the forces at his disposal on Soissons.

Soult moved d'Erlon south of Soissons. His cavalry screen withdrew towards Laon, while the main bodies of cavalry rode to Soissons.

During 25 June, the Prussians pressed on towards the Oise, while Wellington approached St Quentin, which the Prussians had now occupied.

Grouchy moved his cavalry to secure the crossings over the Aisne river. Vandamme again dragged his feet that day, only reaching Rethel. When he arrived in Rheims, Grouchy received an authority from the Provisional Government appointing him commander of all French forces in the north.

Soult reported that he now had around 29,000 men available, including 6,000 cavalry. There was hardly any artillery available. News of Napoleon's abdication led to a further decline in morale. Part of the Guard left for Paris. The National Guardsmen deserted in large numbers and the commandant of Laon did not expect to be able to keep control of his garrison.

On 26 June, the Prussians were poised to march down the Oise valley and seize its important crossings, but several obstacles needed to be overcome before they could do so. The first of these was the fortified town of la Fère, standing as it did on the junction of the Oise and Serre, as well as the Sambre-Oise canal. Blücher recognised the importance of this point and ordered Zieten to seize it. A short bombardment did not break the commandant's will, so he left a screening force there and continued his march.

News came in that the commandant of Soissons was willing to surrender to the Allies and that the townsfolk were strongly royalist in sentiment, but that 10,000 troops from Paris were expected there. Zieten's vanguard immediately moved on Compiègne, shortening the distance to Paris. Bülow started force-marching his troops towards the Oise. Wellington's men had enjoyed a two-day rest, but started moving again, reaching Vermand. Blücher's lead was increasing day by day.

Discipline in Grouchy's force was largely intact, so he decided to try to slow the Allied advance on Paris by threatening its flank. D'Erlon spent the night of 26/27 June around Châtelet, between Soissons and Compiègne. Grouchy ordered him to march to Senlis and stop the Prussian advance. Lacking clear instructions from Paris, Grouchy was acting on his own initiative and was about to join battle with the Prussians.

On 27 June, Blücher instructed Zieten to move through Compiègne and on to Gilocourt, with Thielemann following as far as Compiègne. Bülow was ordered to cross the Oise at Creil and other places, then move on to Senlis and other points. Blücher was pushing his exhausted men hard. At every halt, many of them dropped off to sleep.

Just after the Prussians entered Compiègne at 5am, a French column was reported to be approaching from Soissons. An hour later, French skirmishers deployed into the Compiègne Wood, while an assault column and artillery battery moved up. Their half-hearted attempt to attack the Prussians achieved little, and for the next hour or two, the French covered their withdrawal with a skirmish action. They seemed to be moving south, but the expected assault on Compiègne from that direction did not take place. Instead, d'Erlon continued to withdraw in that direction, while reporting to Grouchy that the Prussians were likely to continue their advance from Compiègne. He clashed with the pursuing Prussian cavalry as he crossed the Automne river at Gilocourt.

Meanwhile, Grouchy was anticipating d'Erlon to move into Compiègne and was expecting Vandamme to arrive. He ordered Reille and the Guard to Nanteuil. Vandamme was sent several messages urging him to expedite his orders energetically so that they could move to cover Paris.

At 1am on 28 June, Pirch II's Brigade surprised and overwhelmed a force of French cavalry and infantry under Lefebvre-Desnoëttes at Villers-Cotterêts, capturing a number of guns and waggons and taking many prisoners. At daybreak, an artillery bombardment put the Guard infantry to flight, with some heading for Paris and others back to Soissons.

Vandamme's cavalry then moved round the flanks of the Prussians, while his infantry engaged them frontally. Weight of numbers prevailed and the Prussians withdrew. Meanwhile, Pirch II tried to work his way around the French flank, but poor roads delayed him. He failed to intercept the French and they continued their march to Paris.

Zieten led some of his cavalry in an attempt to catch up with Grouchy, but was also unsuccessful. Although Grouchy got away, there was nothing he could do to stop the Prussians closing in on Paris.

On 28 June, Bülow moved to Gonesse, with his vanguard approaching St Denis, on the outskirts of Paris. It clashed with French outposts at le Bourget and Stains. Meanwhile, Thielemann moved to support Zieten.

Wellington finally started to accelerate the pace of his march on the French capital, crossing the Somme river at Villecourt on 27 June and moving on to positions 40km to the rear of the Prussians the next day.

On 28 June, the Chamber declared Paris to be in a stage of siege, calling up all old soldiers. Two regiments of the Young Guard were on their way from having quelled the royalist uprising in the Vendée. The Prussian advance was being taken seriously indeed.

Avoiding routes that the Prussians could have intercepted, Grouchy continued to fall back to Paris. By 29 June, most of his men had reached the line of fortifications to the north of the great city. Having brought back a

An artist's dramatic impression of the race of the allied armies to Paris

largely intact army for the defence of the capital, Grouchy felt he had now done his duty and resigned his position. Vandamme was placed in command of all troops on the left bank of the Seine. The same day, the Prussians reached their prize.

Blücher now instructed Bülow to seize St Denis if the French were not holding it. However, they were, so he had to be content with establishing outposts nearby. Preparations were made to throw a bridge across the Seine below Paris. Zieten and Thielemann closed in on the city.

Wellington and Blücher conferred on the evening of 29 June at Gonesse. The Duke requested Blücher to await the arrival of his forces, then to hold his positions north of Paris, while Wellington moved around the west and to the south. The Prussians had, however, started making the first moves in that direction and had seized the bridge over the Seine at St Germain.

After examining the situation on 30 June, it was evident to Blücher that the French were determined to make a stand along the northern perimeter of the city, so rather than engage them here, losing time in which Wellington could close up on him, Blücher decided to screen the north, while moving around the west of the city to take it from the undefended south. He issued the appropriate orders.

Thielemann was the first to start the manoeuvre around Paris, while Zieten and Bülow remained where they were. That afternoon, the French noticed that Thielemann was moving off, so they launched two sorties from St Denis. The fighting continued into the evening.

A bridging train moved on Argenteuil, while on 1 July Thielemann's men crossed the Seine at St Germain. Zieten followed in his trail at night, so the French would not notice his movement. Meanwhile, the French staged another sortie from St Denis.

Wellington moved up to relieve Bülow that afternoon, so Bülow then marched off to Argenteuil, where a temporary bridge was being constructed across the Seine.

Exelmans received news that Prussian hussars were present in the main square of Versailles, so he moved to meet them. A confused skirmish took place in which the Prussians were driven off, losing many killed, wounded or captured. This was the one defeat the Prussians suffered in this stage of the campaign.

On 2 July, Wellington took up positions facing St Denis, while Blücher continued his sweep around the south-west of Paris. The movement was centred on Versailles. French forces moved to meet them and there were several clashes before Thielemann moved into Châtillon. A French request for a ceasefire was declined. Blücher had every intention of taking Paris before agreeing to an end of hostilities.

The next day, the French army made one final show of force before the city capitulated. Vandamme stormed Issy with such determination that Zieten thought he might have to abandon it. However, he was able to hold his positions. The same force of Prussians that fired the first shot of the campaign also fired the last. Later that day, the Convention of Paris was signed. On 7 July, Zieten's men staged a victory parade through Paris. France's capital might have surrendered, but the fortress war went on for several more months.

The northern French fortress belt

The line of fortresses covering the Franco-Netherlands border at this time included, from east to west, Longwy, Bouillon, Sedan, Charleville-Mézières, Givet-Charlemont, Rocroi, Philippeville, Mariembourg, Avesnes, Maubeuge, Landrecies, Le Quesnoy, Condé, Valenciennes and Cambrai. There were also several fortified towns on the route to Paris, including Péronne, la Fère, Laon and Soissons.

Napoleon had chosen their commanders carefully. Most were staunch Bonapartists, who did not want to cooperate with the Allies. The fortresses contained significant supplies of food and ammunition and could have been used as bases for conducting guerrilla warfare along the Allies' lines of communication. They posed a potential threat that needed to be neutralised if not eliminated before victory over Napoleon could be secured. Furthermore, the Prussians wanted to seize these fortresses and demolish them, plundering their stores and weakening France's defences.

While the Prussians continued their race to Paris, Wellington and Blücher met in Catillon on 23 June to discuss how to deal with the fortresses. They decided to divide their areas of operations, with Wellington taking those west of the Sambre river and Blücher those on the Sambre and east of it.

Wellington delegated this work to Prince Frederik of the Netherlands, allocating him the 1st Netherlands Division, the Indian Brigade, along with cavalry and artillery supports.

Prince August of Prussia was given the job of conducting the sieges in the Prussian zone. He was allocated the II Army Corps, the North German Federal Army Corps and the garrison of the fortress of Luxembourg.

The Prussians were much more vigorous in their conduct of the sieges than Wellington. The Duke considered himself to be the liberator of France from Bonaparte and an ally of Louis XVIII. The Prussians, who had suffered years of occupation by the French, saw the matter differently. Wellington was at war with Napoleon, while the Prussians considered themselves to be at war with France, particularly as the provisional government that replaced Napoleon did not prove cooperative. As well as revenge, they wanted to plunder France's resources as compensation for their own losses and see to it that French military power was so weakened that it would no longer be such a threat to Prussian security. Such variances in political objectives led to different military strategies. While Wellington was happy to send Napoleon into exile on St Helena, the Prussians wanted him strung up on the nearest tree. While Wellington was happy to allow any fortresses that declared for Louis XVIII to do so, the Prussians wanted to seize them, take their supplies and if possible blow them up as well.

Le Quesnoy

From 22 June, Prince Frederik invested le Quesnoy, a small fortress southeast of Valenciennes. The next day and on 26 June, he undertook some small, but unsuccessful, demonstrations against the fortress. After an artillery bombardment on 27 June, more forceful assaults were made and the fortress commandant then declared for Louis XVIII, opening his gates to the Netherlanders.

Valenciennes and Condé

The Netherlanders then moved on to Valenciennes, with the Indian Brigade going on to observe the small fort of Condé to the north. Some of the heavy guns in le Quesnoy were brought up and on 1 July a bombardment of the fortress that went on for three days and nights commenced. The citizens of Valenciennes staged an uprising, running up the white flag, but the garrison put them down. The bombardment started again on 7 July and continued until 20 July, when the commandant, General Roy, declared for Louis XVIII, but refused to open the gates to the Allies. They continued to observe the fortress until it capitulated on 12 August.

The events at Condé passed along similar lines.

As the fortresses of Lille, Douai and Bouchain had declared for Louis XVIII, there was no need to besiege them.

Maubeuge

Built in Vauban's earlier style, the fortress of Maubeuge was the strongest on the Sambre river, even if it was in a state of disrepair, with part of the high outer walls having fallen down. There were only two gates, one on the north side; the other on the south-west. One outwork, the Redoubt Mont-la-Croix, covered the north-west corner, another, the Redoubt la Falaise, a star fort, was to the east. Ditches and covered communication trenches linked them to the fortress.

The commandant was General Marie-Victor-Nicolas de Fay, Count de la Tour-Maubourg. Of the roughly 3,000 men garrison, only a few were regular soldiers, most being national guardsmen. But the townsfolk stood behind their commandant, and he had 80 guns and large quantities of ammunition and provisions at his disposal, so taking this fortress was not likely to be easy. Maubeuge blocked the use of the Sambre for shipping, so its capture was important for the Allies.

The Prussian 5th Brigade and some Hanoverian hussars started observing Maubeuge from 20 June. On 24 June, Pirch I, commander of the Prussian II Army Corps, issued orders for its investment, which was undertaken by the 5th and 7th Brigades, the 5th on the left bank, the 7th on the right. Along with supporting troops, this amounted to nearly 10,000 men.

Obviously, the attached brigade artillery was insufficient for the job to hand, so heavier guns were brought up, including 24, 16 and 12 pounders, howitzers and mortars, a total of eighteen pieces. They came along in dribs and drabs, delaying Prince August's intention to seize this fortress quickly, and by 28 June only six were available. Nevertheless, Prince August pressed ahead with his preparations, deploying the brigade artillery and seizing good positions for his batteries on the night of 27/28 June. The next day, the garrison undertook an unsuccessful sortie. The available guns were moved into position during the night of 28/29 June and the bombardment began the next morning, lasting from then into the night. The damage to Maubeuge was severe, with the town being set alight and the church burning down. However, the fortifications were not damaged, so la Tour-Maubourg declined an offer to surrender. The Prussians now needed to reconsider their strategy. After firing nearly 3,000 rounds, they had achieved little. From 30 June, the guns were redeployed and a new plan of attack drawn up.

The Prussians had been digging parallels and batteries around Maubeuge for several days. They now decided to concentrate their efforts on the Falaise Redoubt, attacking it from the east. First, they staged a bluff from the south, hoping to make the French move their guns there.

On 8 July, Wellington's siege train of 38 heavy guns under Colonel Dixon arrived. That night, the assault on the Falaise Redoubt began. Parallels were dug as close as 80 paces from the redoubt and three batteries were prepared for Dixon's nine light mortars. As the tall crops hid this work from the French, it was not interrupted until the morning, when some mortar shells were dropped and musketry opened up. The Allied mortar and sniper fire was so much more effective, that the garrison abandoned its position at 11am, taking its guns with it and falling back into the main fortress.

The same night, a parallel was dug on the opposite side of the Sambre, about 300 paces from the Mont-la-Croix Redoubt. From here, the Prussian guns decimated the French garrison.

On the night of 10/11 July, further batteries were constructed to the east of Maubeuge, but this work was delayed by heavy French fire. Further batteries were then constructed on the opposite bank for heavy mortars. A French sortie was repelled, but the work could not be completed.

The bombardment commenced on the morning of 11 July. The French counter-battery fire was so effective that the British 24-pounders were almost forced to cease firing. During the course of the morning, the French abandoned the Mont-la-Croix Redoubt.

The bombardment of Maubeuge continued into the afternoon. However, at 4pm, the commandant raised the white flag and requested terms for surrender, which were agreed the next morning. The regulars were allowed to leave the fortress with full honours of war, while the National Guard was sent home. The Prussians occupied the fortress on the morning of 14 July, taking a considerable amount of booty, particularly small-arms and ammunition, from the town's factory.

Landrecies

Landrecies was also on the Sambre, and as such was a further obstacle to this line of communication. Constructed in Vauban style, it was relatively small, just a few hundred paces wide. A large hornwork protected the suburb on the left bank, while the Sambre fed the ditches. One gate stood in the south-east corner, another in the north-west, in the hornwork. Trees were growing on the glacis, and houses, gardens and hedges blocked the line of sight, and none of these obstructions had been cleared. Colonel Plaige commanded the garrison of 2,000 National Guardsmen, mainly Bonapartists. He had 45 heavy guns and a large supply of ammunition at his disposal. The townsfolk were mainly royalists.

Elements of the Prussian IV Army Corps started the investment of Landrecies on 22 June, being replaced by the 6th Brigade two days later. Sporadic firing took place, but there was no serious bombardment for a while. Louis XVIII appointed a new commandant, who arrived on 6 July, but Plaige refused to acknowledge him. Even the news of the fall of Maubeuge did not make him change his mind. However, once Maubeuge was in Allied hands, more artillery and troops became available for use against Landrecies. These started coming up on 13 July.

Major-General von Krafft now took charge of the siege operations and the eastern side of the fortress was selected as the point of attack, while the western hornwork was designated for a feint. On 17 July, the last of the guns required arrived. These included twenty-six captured French pieces and thirty British. On the night of 19/20 July, a parallel was dug close to the hornwork. The French opened fire on it the following morning. At 11am the white flag was raised and the commandant offered to surrender to Louis XVIII, which the Prussians declined.

The siege now continued with the Prussians constructing five batteries behind the parallel in which ten 24-pounders and nine mortars were placed. They also dug another parallel to the east of Landrecies. The bombardment commenced at 7am on 21 July, being aimed at the gate and the bridge linking the town with the hornwork. As most of the garrison was at roll-call, there was little counter-fire. Louis' appointee seized the opportunity and led the townsfolk to Plaige's headquarters and demanded he capitulate. Plaige obliged, although this was against the wishes of the garrison.

The capitulation of Landrecies allowed shipping to move from the Sambre via the Ouse to the Seine. An important line of supply was now open.

Mariembourg

Mariembourg was a small rectangular fort just over 400 paces wide. A wet ditch ran around its perimeter and its wall was four metres high and one metre thick. The surrounding heights overlooked its low earth lunettes.

The Prussians invested this fort from 24 June. The commandant refused to surrender, so the howitzers of the 8th Brigade commenced a bombardment. A sortie undertaken by the garrison of 350 men was repelled. Most of the 8th Brigade then moved on to Givet, leaving behind a small observation force. Only a few minor skirmishes took place in the following days.

On 26 July, the Prussians again called on the commandant to surrender, but he declined. On the night of 26/27 July, a parallel was dug and two batteries constructed. The work had not been finished by daybreak and was then interrupted by fire from the French. During the course of the morning, the Prussians fired shells into the fort, but these had little effect. Prince August now sent for heavy artillery from Philippeville, but at 3pm the garrison raised the white flag, having used up all its ammunition. The Prussians occupied the fort on 30 July and demolished it.

Philippeville

Philippeville was one of the strongest fortresses in this theatre. It straddled the most direct line of communication between the Sambre and Meuse and as such was a considerable nuisance to the Allies. The fortifications were

Philippeville. The only part of the fortifications standing in 1815 that remains today has been made into a chapel.

well sited on a hill that towered over the entire area. Much of the northern side and parts of the southern approaches were marshy and only on the western side was there any cover for the attacker. Vauban had extended and modernised the fortifications and they were in good condition, able to withstand a bombardment. The stony ground made it difficult for the attacker to dig trenches and earthworks.

The commandant was General Cassaigne and he had 1,700 men available – a mixture of National Guardsmen, regulars and customs officials. The fortress was equipped with fifty-one heavy cannon. The townsfolk largely supported the commandant.

The first Prussians arrived on 23 June, but only screened the fortress lightly. From 18 July, more besiegers started to arrive, sealing off the area.

Heavy siege equipment was brought up from Maubeuge and Landrecies, this being completed by 6 August. In all, eighty-six heavy cannon, howitzers and mortars were placed around Philippeville and nearly 50,000 rounds of artillery ammunition were made available.

The decision was made to concentrate efforts on the western side and southern bastion and the construction of the first parallel commenced on the night of 7/8 August. Despite rotating the work parties, little progress was made, as the stony ground was difficult to dig. Eventually, six batteries were constructed and a number of howitzers and mortars brought up. The 24-pounders could not be deployed due to a lack of cover in the rocky terrain.

At 6am the fog lifted and the defenders opened a heavy fire against the parallels. A ceasefire was called at noon, when Cassaigne unsuccessfully attempted to negotiate a surrender. At 3pm the bombardment recommenced, setting light to several parts of the fortress, particularly in the barrack block behind the selected bastion. This fire led to resistance collapsing at this point. At 7pm the capitulation of the fortress was offered and accepted, so the construction of further parallels ceased. The Prussians took control of the western gate the next morning and the remainder of the fortress on 10 August. Some of the besieging forces now moved on to Rocroi.

Rocroi

Rocroi was a small, Vauban-style fortress that was just 350 paces wide. Blocking the only direct line of communication between the Prussians besieging Givet and the North German Federal Army corps at Mézières, it was an annoying obstacle that needed to be removed. The fortifications were in good order and various improvements had been made. The ditches were dry, but contained rainwater. There were two gates, one to the north-west; the other to the west. General Projean commanded about 1,500 men with thirty-five guns and intended to fight. The major and various officers were not so keen.

The first Prussian observation troops arrived on 29 June. Various bodies of troops came and went from 1 to 29 July. There were several clashes between the garrison and the besiegers.

Prince August arrived on 10 August, being greeted by a French sortie that evening. The siege was now moving into its hot phase. After due consideration, he decided to attack from the west, concentrating on the bastion nearest the west gate, as the houses and gardens on this steep slope provided cover. The siege artillery started arriving from Philippeville on 11 August. By 14 August, thirty-three heavy howitzers and mortars had arrived, but there was little ammunition and a lack of entrenching tools and equipment. Nevertheless, the construction of the parallels and batteries went ahead and fire from the fortress artillery on 14 and 15 August did not interrupt this work. Indeed, a firework display celebrating Napoleon's birthday on 14 August provided the diggers with extra illumination. By then, an approach trench had been constructed to within 150 paces of the covered way in front of the point of the selected bastion. A parallel was then dug and five batteries constructed.

The bombardment commenced at 7am on 16 August, just after the fog had cleared. The fortress artillery returned the fire, inflicting severe damage to one battery. However, the Prussians concentrated their fire so effectively that the magazine at the west gate was on the point of collapse. At 9am negotiations for surrender commenced, and at noon, the fortress capitulated. However, the townsfolk and part of the garrison objected to this, taking over much of the fortress until the appearance of three battalions of Prussian infantry pacified them. Part of the artillery captured was then sent on to Givet.

Givet-Charlemont

This fortress blocked the Meuse river, the shortest line of communication from Prussian Rhineland to northern France. Blücher's supply route was currently running via Liège and Namur, which was the long way round. Moreover, the routes south of Luxembourg were shortly to be taken up by the movement of the Austrian and Russian forces about to commence their advance into France, so there was a degree of urgency here.

This fortress consisted of a series of works running along the northern bank of the Meuse from Charlemont to Grand Givet, then south of the Meuse at Petit Givet and the Mont d'Haurs. There were also several outworks, including the Fort Condé to the north-west and the Fort des Vignes to the east. Vauban had constructed the existing works, although there had been fortifications at this strategic point for centuries. These works are regarded as some of Vauban's best.

The fortifications enhanced the topographical features of this position, standing on a wedge-shaped ridge that rose as much as 120 metres above the Meuse valley. The northern side was very steep, the southern descended sharply to the Meuse, and the eastern was a sheer cliff. Most of the fortress's ditches were cut in rock. Much of the ground was stony, making it difficult for a besieger to dig here.

The Fort Condé was connected to Charlemont by a covered way around 400 metres long. It has been hollowed out of solid rock. An entrenched camp was situated on the plateau of the Mont d'Haurs. A road connected it with Petit Givet, which lay at the foot of its rocky face. The Fort des Vignes covered the roads to Dinant and Luxembourg. The old earth redoubt north of the Fort des Vignes was garrisoned in daytime.

A deep, wet ditch covered the bastions of Grand Givet. The Houille river had been diverted around the northern side of Petit Givet and a single bridge connected Petit Givet with Grand Givet. In all, this position was ideal for the defence.

General Count Burke was the commandant and he had just over 3,000 men available, well below the 11,000 considered necessary for the defence. Burke raised the white flag over the fortress on hearing of events elsewhere. He declared himself for Louis XVIII, but the Prussians, wanting to control this strategic point, did not accept that. Instead, they set about besieging this fortress. Due to their commitments elsewhere and the fact that they would not be allowed to use Wellington's siege train against a fortress that had declared for Louis XVIII, this would take them some time.

Elements of Bose's Brigade arrived in the area on 25 June, but they were too few to do anything but observe the fortress. More of this brigade arrived on 19 July, after the fall of Philippeville and Rocroi. The last of it came up on 24 July, along with those parts of Krafft's Brigade that had been at Rocroi. Once the final elements of Krafft's Brigade arrived on 10 August, the siege proper began.

On 20 August, Blücher allocated further troops to the besieging forces in the shape of two Hessian brigades from the North German Army Corps. The Hessians were not too keen on being placed under Prussian command, as they felt this compromised their independence.

Prince August then took stock of the situation and worked out a plan of action. He reported to Blücher that due to the lack of artillery, ammunition, tools and equipment, he considered it impossible to stage an assault on these fortifications and instead negotiated for free passage of the Meuse. Blücher, pressed by a lack of supplies to maintain his troops in the area, overruled the Prince, demanding he storm the fortress without delay. All the Prince had in his favour was superiority in numbers, so he decided on a course of action.

Thanks to the size of the force at his disposal, the Prince would be able to threaten several points simultaneously, forcing the commandant to spread his men out thinly to cover all threats. Prince August would then storm one point and hopefully seize it. He decided to take the Fort des Vignes, while laying diversionary fire on both Charlemont and Givet. Once in control of this fort, he could then move on Petit Givet and the Mont d'Haurs. All available guns and ammunition were brought up. By 6 September, he had 129 pieces of heavy artillery available, along with 26,000 rounds of ammunition, as well as equipment taken from other Prussian army corps. The Prince now had sufficient resources to storm Petit Givet.

Meanwhile, Prussian sappers prepared for the siege, building several temporary bridges in the area to facilitate the movement of men and equipment. The outnumbered garrison did little other than watch this.

The Prussians made their first move on the night of 2/3 September, when sixty infantry took over the old redoubt after the garrison had withdrawn for the night. Returning the next morning, the French were surprised to find the Prussians there and fell back. A bombardment of the lost positions was largely ineffective and Prussian reinforcements arrived. After two hours of fighting, the French pulled back.

The Prussians now dug parallels and batteries to provide covering fire for their assault on the Fort des Vignes and Petit Givet. A total of sixty-two artillery pieces of varying types and calibres were allocated to this section of the front, the first of which were deployed on the night of 8/9 September.

Burke had, however, already recognised the danger and commenced negotiations for a partial withdrawal of his forces. On 11 September, the Prussians occupied Grand and Petit Givet along with the Mont d'Haurs. They then went on to prepare an assault on Charlemont, constructing several batteries and placing a mine under the main wall of Charlemont. On 20 September, Burke indicated he was about to hinder this work with a bombardment, but received orders for an end of hostilities that day. Despite that, Burke did not hand over his charge and the siege continued until 30 November, after peace had been declared. Russian troops then occupied it.

Sedan

On 16 June, the North German Army Corps had been ordered to march to Sedan. On 22 June, the Anhalt-Thuringian Brigade with supporting cavalry and artillery was detached and sent to Bouillon (see below). Two days later, the remainder of the corps was closing on Vandamme's line of retreat. It clashed with French patrols. On 26 June, the North Germans started to reach Sedan, moving down both sides of the Meuse valley. The available artillery fired on the town, persuading its commandant, Baron Choisy, to abandon the town and its considerable stock of supplies and withdraw into the castle. He surrendered on 20 August.

Bouillon

In 1814, the French had occupied the town of Bouillon in the Semois valley, which was an independent duchy. Fire from howitzers of the North

German Army Corps did not persuade its commandant, General Bonnichon, to surrender, so not being in a position to storm it, the Lippe-Waldeck Regiment was left behind to blockade it, while the remainder of the Anhalt-Thuringian Brigade left for Sedan.

On 21 July, the commandant indicated his willingness to hand over the fort to Louis XVIII, but the Allies rejected this because Bouillon was in an area of territory now allocated to the Kingdom of the Netherlands. When Bonnichon refused to open his gates to the new owners, Netherlands troops arrived on 14 August and the garrison surrendered on 23 August.

Mézières

The fortress of Mézières covered a considerable area and included the arms and powder manufactory of Charleville. This was a prize that the Prussians did not want to ignore, so on 28 June, Jagow's Brigade of Zieten's Corps started to blockade it.

The works consisted of five sections. First, there was the old town of Mézières, the centre of the fortifications covering two bridges over the Meuse. Then there were the fortifications of St Julien, on the peninsula to the west of the old town. To the east of the old town stood the citadel, with its fleches designed to protect the town's water supply. Finally, there were two sets of works designed to cover the bridgeheads to the north and south. High walls and supporting works protected three sides of the town of Charleville. The Meuse ran along the fourth side.

On 11 June, the commandant General Lemoine arrived and set about raising a garrison by mobilising the local National Guard around a core of customs officers. He was able to man his charge with 3,000 men, and had sixty fortress pieces at his disposal. General Laplanche commanded Charleville and had around 1,000 National Guardsmen available.

On 28 June, Lt-General von Hake, formerly a brigade commander in the Prussian IV Army Corps, took control of the investing forces here. He deployed the Thuringians on the right bank of the Meuse and the Hessians on the left.

The next day, a mixed force of Hessians and Prussians drew up to attack Charleville. Calls for surrender were rejected, so fire was opened. At first, this had little effect and the fire the defenders returned was more effective. A storming party then assaulted the palisades. After the gate was destroyed, the town was entered and most of the garrison surrendered. The Hessians took the opportunity of resupplying themselves with firearms from the town's stores.

Once Charleville had fallen, the townsfolk of Mézières grew restless and removed the tricolour from the flagpole, but Lemoine managed to regain control of the situation. A lack of ammunition prevented the besiegers from exploiting the opportunity. More guns and ammunition were brought up in the second half of July. Nevertheless, the defenders rained fire on the German soldiers digging batteries in Charleville and Mohon. On 24 July, a French sortie was driven off and the next morning Lemoine surprised the besiegers by attacking through the tall crops. The main column moved on Mohon, the two smaller ones on Charleville and St Laurent. German reinforcements moved up from the rear and drove back the French columns, over 1,000 men strong.

Starting at dawn on 26 July, the besiegers bombarded Mézières non-stop for twenty-four hours, setting light to parts of the town. The defenders returned the fire effectively, setting light to parts of Charleville.

As talks between Louis XVIII's envoy and Lemoine proved fruitless, Hake set about preparing to storm Mézières. Fifty guns were brought up and bridges built at Warcq and Prix, and the assault was to take place on St Julien. On 31 July, a battalion of Oldenburgers marched to the fleche to the east of the citadel, but that and subsequent attempts to hold this area failed due to the heavy fire from the defenders.

On the night of 6/7 August, an assault on the fortifications at St Julien failed, but the attackers maintained their hold on the peninsula, later building earthworks and batteries, including one parallel 500 paces from the western hornwork. The guns they brought up opened fire early on 9 August. That evening, Lemoine agreed to withdraw into the citadel with 800 men on 13 August. The besiegers continued to extend their ring of parallels and batteries, despite Lemoine's protests. With Prussian guns deployed in houses just 12 metres from the citadel, Lemoine surrendered on 3 September.

Prussian losses amounted to two officers and nineteen men killed; seven officers, twenty-three NCOs and 136 men wounded.

Montmédy

Two small fortresses blocked the line of communication that ran through the Ardennes from Luxembourg. One was Montmédy, the other Longwy. On hearing that peace was about to break out, Prince August decided to first take Montmédy, the weaker one.

The fortress of Montmédy was situated on a rock in the Chiers valley. Its walls were 7 metres high and 1½ metres thick and also protected the road from the town to the fortress. There were a number of outworks around the walled town of Médy, which had three gates. The commandant was General Laurent, who had a mixture of regulars, veterans, customs officers, gendarmes and National Guardsmen at his disposal.

The besiegers consisted of various detachments from the North German Army Corps. During the night of 4/5 September, they took the heights north of the Chiers and drove off a counterattack made the next morning. Hake brought up reinforcements and, during the night of 11/12 September, seized the reservoir that supplied the town with its drinking water. Under pressure to take Montmédy rapidly and lacking the necessary manpower to storm it, Hake decided to seize Médy and cut off the entire water supply to the fortress. A mixed force of German troops closed in for the assault on the night of 12/13 September. Scaling the town walls at 2.30am on 13 September, they took the garrison completely by surprise. The French fell back to the fortress while the attackers destroyed the wells. From dawn, the fortress fired into the town, but at 9am it was agreed to allow the inhabitants to leave. The next night, five further batteries were constructed. Negotiations for surrender started on 16 September and terms were agreed three days later. On 22 September, the fortress was handed over.

Longwy

Lt-General Prince of Hesse-Homburg commanded the garrison of the fortress of Luxembourg that consisted in the large part of Prussian militia. Ordered to seize Longwy, most of Hesse-Homburg's force marched off, arriving there during the night of 1/2 July. The accompanying artillery immediately opened up fire on Longwy from the north-east, while the infantry assaulted it from the south. They were driven back after having taken this position, so more artillery was brought up. A battery was built on the Mont du Chat by 9 July and from here the fortress was bombarded for three days.

Meanwhile, a relief force approached from Metz and Thionville, arriving during the night of 11/12 July and taking the besiegers by surprise. The Prussians were driven off with some loss and the siege lifted.

Towards the end of July, the Prussian VI Army Corps started its march into France, allowing Hesse-Homburg to invest Longwy again. His force now included a mixture of soldiers from various German states, together with twenty-six siege guns. More guns arrived later, but were not used.

In the night of 10/11 August, the attackers' earthworks reached from 800 to 1,000 paces from the fortress. Three battalions of Prussian militia deployed on the Mont du Chat, while another two deployed to the south of the fortress. The reserves moved into position.

The commandant of the fortress asked to be allowed to take instructions from Paris and Louis XVIII sent him orders to disband the National Guard, but to continue to hold the fortress with his regulars if they agreed. They did, so the ceasefire was ended and a bombardment commenced during the night of 9/10 September. The fire of the defenders took its toll until the observer in the church spire was dislodged.

During the night of 13/14 September, Prussian infantry broke into the fortress from the south, but part of the garrison took refuge in the blockhouse. They surrendered only after the Prussians set light to this building. That evening, the fortress capitulated on the understanding the garrison could leave for Metz. More supplies and booty fell into Prussian hands.

The war of 1815 was drawing to an end.

Chapter Eight

The Four Armies

Napoleonic warfare

The face of battle underwent a number of changes in the period from 1792 to 1815, the most significant of these being to the size of the armies involved. While Frederick the Great fought his battles with 50,000 men, the Battle of the Nations that took place in Leipzig in October 1813 involved half a million. Although military technology had hardly changed in the previous two centuries, the structures of the armies using the smoothbore muzzle-loading flintlock musket developed to allow such large forces to be handled with relative ease.

The first of these developments was the evolution of the army corps, a body of all arms – infantry, cavalry and artillery – that could move and fight independently. An army consisted of several such corps. The army commander now no longer had to concern himself with the minutiae of the entire army, he merely controlled the movements of the corps, which facilitated the command and control of the larger armies characteristic of this period. What was important was the development of a uniformly trained general staff to manage the functioning of all components of such armies.

Napoleon did not have such a general staff and this weakness caused communication problems with Marshal Ney on 16 June and Marshal Grouchy on 18 June that cost him the campaign. Had the command structure been made clear to all involved, and had initiative been allowed, then d'Erlon would not have spent 16 June marching pointlessly between the two battlefields and Grouchy might well have marched to the sound of the guns on 18 June.

Wellington also did not have a uniformly trained staff, as the education of staff officers in the British army was still in its infancy in 1815. Furthermore, a coalition army with contingents from various nations could hardly be trained to a uniform philosophy. Wellington's style was autocratic and he micromanaged his force. While this caused him considerable problems on 15 and 16 June, his great ability as a tactical commander came to the fore on 18 June and played a considerable role in the Allied victory. Fortunately for Wellington, the Netherlanders' high command was able to use its initiative and its actions in holding Quatre Bras on 15 June and seeing that reinforcements were on their way on 16 June gave Wellington his opportunity for fame at Waterloo.

Of all the armies of this period, it was perhaps the Prussians that best analysed the developments in warfare in recent years and set about optimising their military structures. Blücher's army was, in terms of the quality of the manpower and equipment, probably the worst the Prussians ever fielded. Nevertheless, it was able to quickly recover from the defeat at Ligny and only two days later made the attack in Napoleon's right rear at Plancenoit that decided not only the Battle of Waterloo, but also the campaign. It was thanks to a uniformly trained general staff that this was possible.

Each army corps consisted of a number of divisions – for historical reasons known as brigades in the Prussian army at this time. These divisions contained a number of battalions of infantry and often had supporting units of cavalry and batteries of artillery attached. The army corps also often included a cavalry and artillery reserve. Napoleon also had several cavalry corps available and enjoyed a significant superiority in terms of both numbers and quality in his mounted arm.

The bulk of the foot soldiers of this period consisted of line infantry. The standard tactical unit was the battalion, which consisted of several companies. These companies would normally be drawn up in lines of two or three men deep, standing shoulder-to-shoulder, or in close order. The battalions were generally deployed either in line, column or square.

In line, the companies normally stood next to each other. This formation brought the maximum firepower available to bear on its target and was generally favoured for the defence. The line was unwieldy as an offensive formation, particularly as the rapid growth in the size of armies during the Revolutionary and Napoleonic Wars resulted in a dilution of the training given.

The column, which normally consisted of the companies drawn up behind each other, was the preferred formation for movement on the field of

Prussian Landwehr. This particular militiaman is wearing a British-made shako, part of the supplies Britain delivered to Prussian in 1813.

Prussian Landwehr. This man is a veteran of the Waterloo Campaign (he is wearing the campaign medal) and one of the troops occupying Paris after Waterloo.

battle. It was often used offensively, charging into the enemy positions. Individual company and platoon columns were often used in the street fighting that characterised many battles in this period. As the limited frontage of the column did not optimise the battalion's firepower, this was usually compensated for by deploying part of the battalion in a skirmish line, to its fore. Either the third rank of the companies or specialist light companies were used for this purpose. Skirmishers fought in pairs – one loading, one firing.

The square was used largely as a defensive formation against cavalry. It could be formed either from a line, in which case the companies of the battalion folded back to form a hollow box, or from a column, in which case the rear ranks about faced and the flank files faced outwards. Squares were normally used statically, with the battalion squares of a brigade or division being deployed in a chequerboard formation. This was to give overlapping fire and avoid friendly fire. Infantry sometimes moved in squares, particularly when they had no cavalry support.

There were also units of specialist infantry, some light, others heavy. The light infantry were used to skirmish on the battlefield, or in patrols and vanguards when off it. Some light infantry were armed with rifled weapons – slower to load, but more accurate than the muskets of the line. Selected men were placed together in heavy infantry battalions, such as grenadiers, and were often the army's last reserve, delivering the final blow in a battle.

The cavalry was divided into two basic types – heavy and light – although there were various shades of grey in between. The heavy cavalry usually consisted of large men, often wearing body armour, on big, strong horses. They were most used on the field of battle, where their weight could ride down a line of infantry, particularly one that was broken. The best-known type of heavy cavalry was Napoleon's cuirassiers. Dragoons were also regarded as heavy cavalry. They too consisted of big men on large horses, but were not normally armoured. Originating from mounted infantry, they also carried carbines, a shortened musket. They were also used mainly in a battlefield role. The light cavalry consisted of hussars and lancers, although the British cavalry included light dragoons and the French had its chasseurs à cheval. Hussars were small men on nimble horses used for patrols, pursuit, outpost duties and occasionally as battle cavalry. Lancers were armed with a spear-like weapon.

The standard tactical unit of the cavalry was a squadron, normally around 100 men. The squadrons normally drew up in two or three ranks. A regiment could deploy its squadrons in line or column, depending on circumstances. Cavalry could also be used in a skirmish role, with men being drawn from a particular troop for the purpose. They too fought in pairs using their firearms.

There were several types of artillery, some of which were used in a battlefield role. The standard type of artillery was the foot artillery, used to give the infantry supporting fire. Most of these guns were lighter pieces, designed for mobility. Heavy guns were also used, particularly as part of a grand battery bombarding the enemy in preparation for the infantry assault. Batteries of horse artillery – lighter pieces towed by more horses with all its crew mounted – were often attached to cavalry brigades and divisions to give them mobile, supporting fire.

There were two basic types of artillery piece used in the field. One was a cannon, a tube made of bronze or iron on a wheeled carriage, used for direct fire. The other was a howitzer, which had a shorter tube and was used for indirect fire. These tubes were smoothbore and had a touchhole at the nearest end though which the charge was ignited.

The cannon mainly fired round-shot, that is, spheres of metal. These were fired over open sights at a distance of several hundred paces. A good gunner sought to achieve as much roll-on as possible, getting the ball to land just in front of its target, then roll through it. At shorter ranges, canister was used. This consisted of a tin box containing small pieces of metal. The box would burst open when fired, scattering its contents over a shorter distance.

The howitzer mainly fired shells, hollow spheres containing explosives or incendiaries that were set off by crude fuses. It was used for indirect fire or to ignite buildings. It could also be used to fire canister when required.

The guns were mounted on carriages drawn on a small ammunition wagon known as a limber. The limber contained only a limited supply of ammunition. Larger supplies were carried in accompanying wagons known as caissons.

The standard tactical unit of the artillery was the battery, normally six to eight pieces, of which most were cannon and two were often howitzers. One or two batteries were attached to most brigades or divisions, while larger reserves, particularly of the heavier pieces, were held at corps or army level.

Heavier pieces were used in siege warfare, normally larger cannon, howitzers and mortars. The larger cannon were used to blast holes in the walls of fortresses, while the howitzers would throw shells and often incendiaries over the walls into the more vulnerable parts of the fortress town, the wooden residential buildings behind the walls, hoping to set them alight. The fortress artillery also included larger cannon, howitzers and mortars designed to destroy the besiegers' fortifications and earthworks, as well as to lob shells into their entrenchments.

When conducting sieges, the attacker would normally first invest or blockade the fortifications in question. If insufficient forces were available, then they would merely be screened or observed. The first phase of the assault would consist of digging saps or trenches towards the fortifications. At various places at right angles to the saps, parallels would be cut. These are lines of trenches that run parallel with the walls of the fortifications. Parts of the parallels would be extended into batteries; that is positions where siege artillery could be placed. From there, the walls, the fortifications, or the town within them, would be bombarded until the enemy surrendered. A breach in the walls was often considered sufficient cause for the defender to capitulate.

A battle consisted of a number of phases. Normally, the artillery would prepare the ground for an infantry assault with a heavy bombardment of the position to be attacked. A line of skirmishers would precede the infantry columns, testing the enemy's resolve. If the infantry succeeded in breaking through the enemy line, cavalry would be used to exploit this and pursue the beaten enemy.

Napoleon's Army

When Napoleon first abdicated in 1814, Europe had been at war for a generation. Suddenly, a large group of men were confronted with peace for the first time in living memory and many had a problem adjusting to civilian life. In France particularly there were many malcontents itching to take up the sword again. When Napoleon returned to France from Elba in

March 1815, he knew he had a hard core of men he could rely on, around which a new army could be formed. This body of veterans gave Napoleon an advantage over his enemies.

Too many of Napoleon's senior commanders had found themselves lucrative sinecures in the army of the restored Bourbons. They had made the change from Bonapartist to royalist without apparent difficulty. Many had little problem changing back, but the army did not trust such turncoats. The hard core of veterans anticipated treachery from its officers. While Napoleon had a cadre of experienced infantry, cavalry and artillery, his hold over this fine army was fragile.

Recruiting new men to join the army was fraught with difficulties. While manpower was raised through conscription, many resisted this, generally through war-weariness or royalist conviction. There were local uprisings in France, particularly in the Vendée.

The hardest of the hard core was Napoleon's personal troops, the Imperial Guard. This force was almost an army within an army, consisting of infantry, cavalry and artillery. The most prestigious of these were the infantry battalions of the Old Guard, the élite of the élite. Battalions of Young Guard, the pick of the class of conscripts, were also raised. In total, three regiments of Old and six of Young Guard, each of two battalions of four companies, were formed. A fourth regiment of Old Guard, consisting of just one battalion, was also raised. The cavalry consisted of twenty-six squadrons in four regiments, one of horse grenadiers, one of dragoons, one of chasseurs and one of lancers. The Guard artillery was made up of seventeen batteries.

Each of the ninety regiments of line infantry had a paper-strength of three battalions. Each battalion had six companies, four of the centre, or line, known as fusiliers; one of voltigeurs, or light; and one of grenadiers, or heavy. The fifteen regiments of light infantry had a similar organisation, with the fusiliers being called chasseurs and the grenadiers being known as carabineers. Only some of the regiments actually fielded three battalions in 1815; most had just two available.

The infantry fought in three ranks, with the grenadiers on the right and the voltigeurs on the left. The battalion attack column was formed in double company columns by the centre. The grenadiers and voltigeurs could be detached, deploying one section as skirmishers with the other in support. A square had two companies on two sides, and one each on the other two sides.

The heavy or reserve cavalry consisted of two regiments of carabineers and twelve of cuirassiers. The dragoons and lancers made up the battle cavalry, while the light cavalry consisted of fifteen regiments of chasseurs à cheval and seven of hussars. Each regiment consisted of four squadrons, each squadron of two companies. The first squadron in each regiment was also known as the élite squadron.

The foot artillery batteries contained six cannon, either 6 or 12-pounders, and two howitzers. The horse batteries had just four 6 pounders and two howitzers.

Blücher's Army

In terms of the quality of the manpower, equipment and training, the Prussian Army of the Lower Rhine was the worst fielded by Prussia in the entire Revolutionary and Napoleonic Wars. Yet it was this army that marched the most, fought the most and bled the most, making the largest contribution to the Allied victory in 1815. This was due largely to the quality of its leadership.

Many of the crack units of the Prussian army were deployed in other theatres, particularly the guards, the grenadiers and the heavy cavalry. Prussia had come close to conflict over the spoils of war with its erstwhile and current allies, and was keeping a careful eye on Austria, particularly because of the Saxon question. The units deployed in the Netherlands contained a smattering of veterans, but were made up largely of untried militia, much of which came from the newly acquired western provinces that had only a year or two ago been under French rule for a generation. The Saxon contingent allocated to the Prussian army had already been sent home in disgrace after a rebellion in May 1815, and other units were considered potentially unreliable. Of the line regiments, several were new formations taken from various free corps and legions that had been raised at the end of the Napoleonic Wars and could hardly be considered regular troops. Much of the cavalry were also new formations, with their squadrons often having come from different origins and wearing different uniforms, which affected their performance.

The Napoleonic Wars had all but bankrupted Prussia and by 1815 everything was in short supply. There was insufficient clothing for the army, meaning what was available was issued, leading to a lack of uniformity. There was a shortage of equipment, with firearms from several nations in use, causing a quartermaster's nightmare. And even where firearms were available, there was not enough ammunition. Some men had empty cartridges in their pouches; others were told to take their ammunition supply from the dead on the field of battle. If that was not bad enough, then unlike the British, the Prussians were not able to pay their hosts in the Netherlands for supplies, and nobody attached much value to a Prussian promissory note, so food was in short supply. Worse still, once the Prussian army went on the march in the blistering heat of 15 to 18 June 1815, there was such a serious shortage of drinking water that the men were dropping dead of heat exhaustion. By all normal means of ascertaining the fighting value of such a force, this army was not fit for combat. It was to end up doing most of the fighting.

Each army corps consisted of four brigades or infantry, the equivalent of divisions in other armies, with the reserve cavalry and artillery attached to the corps. Most brigades also had cavalry and artillery attached. Companies of schützen (sharpshooters) were attached to some brigades. A brigade consisted of nine battalions and was normally drawn up in three waves, the first consisting of two of fusiliers, the second of four of musketeers and the third of the three remaining battalions. The artillery and supporting cavalry were deployed according to circumstances.

A regiment of line infantry consisted of three battalions, two of musketeers (line) and one of fusiliers (light). The militia regiments also consisted of three battalions, the most suitable being selected for light duties and designated fusiliers. Each infantry battalion consisted of four companies. The third rank of all battalions could be detached into skirmish platoons and used for special duties. The attack column was the favoured formation on the field of battle, this being formed by the centre in double company columns. A skirmish line normally preceded it. A square was formed by closing up the ranks, with the rear and side files about facing.

Most cavalry regiments were four squadrons strong, although some only had three.

A battery of artillery normally consisted of six cannon, either 6 or 12-pounders, and two howitzers.

The Federal German Army

The Congress of Vienna re-established a German Confederation to replace the First Reich that had come to an end in 1806. The two largest states in the new confederation were Austria and Prussia, both of whom provided substantial numbers of troops organised into several army corps and so fielded their own armies. The military contingents of the smaller states were organised into army corps based on the regions of Germany from which they originated. Each of these corps was part of the Federal German Army. Only one of these corps, the North German Federal Army Corps, saw active service in the Waterloo Campaign.

This corps consisted of the contingents from Oldenburg, Anhalt, the Thuringian principalities and the Electorate of Hesse. Initially a Prussian,

General Kleist von Nollendorf, commanded it. When he fell ill, another Prussian, Lt-General von Hake, replaced him. In all, these contingents made up three brigades of infantry (two Hessian and the Anhalt-Thuringian Brigade), one cavalry brigade (Hessian) and two batteries of artillery (Hessian). It was a mixed bunch of men, some well trained, armed and equipped, others lacking all the basics required to function as a military force.

Chapter Nine

Tour Guide

Ligny to Wavre

The appropriate place to start a tour of this aspect of the Waterloo Campaign would be from the Ferme du Moulin near Brye, site of Blücher's battle headquarters on 16 June. This farm is situated south of the junction of the N93 Nivelles to Namur road at les trois Burettes. Taking this road into and through the village of Brye, the farm stands on the right, just outside the village. The exact location of the mill is a subject that is often disputed, but the map commissioned by Captain William Siborne for the atlas published in 1844 shows where it stood. Close to here that evening, Blücher was lying injured under his horse, having led the final, but unsuccessful, charge of the day in a vain attempt to halt Napoleon's last attack. The centre of the Prussian position was now broken, and much of the army headed back through Tilly and Mellery to Wavre. There is nothing along the route that indicates the Prussians were ever here, but various monuments and signs indicate that Napoleon's men moved through the area.

On the N93, just north of Brye, is the site of the farm of les trois Burettes, where Napoleon is said to have given Grouchy instructions to pursue the Prussians.

The main axis is the N4, the main road from Namur to Brussels, particularly the section from Gembloux to Wavre. Grouchy's forces moved in this general direction in pursuit of the Prussians on 17 and 18 June. Off this road 2km to the right in Walhain-Saint-Paul is the Evilard farm. Grouchy stopped here for a while on 18 June, when it was the house of Notary Hollert. The sign on the wall of the farm next to the chapel reads, '18 June 1815/Marshal Grouchy was stationed here/while Waterloo was rising up in arms.' At the time of writing, the farm was undergoing restoration work and the sign had yet to be fixed in a permanent place.

Going back onto the N4 and heading for Wavre, one crosses the Pont du Christ. The plaque on one of its walls reads, 'On 18 June 1815 this bridge was the focal point of a battle between the troops of Grouchy and Blücher.' From there, it is a short walk into the centre of town, where there are several places of interest. These include the Church of Saint-Jean-Baptiste in the Place Cardinal Mercer, where a cannonball can been seen inside in

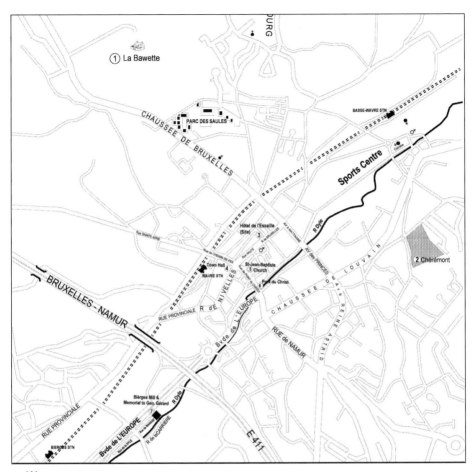

Wavre

the fourth pillar from the right. It is said to originate from the battle of 18/19 June. Close by on the Place de l'Hôtel de Ville (formerly Place des Carmes and Marché aux Bestes), is the Town Hall. It was then a Carmelite convent, and on 18/19 June, it served as a field hospital. It is worth picking up one of the free maps of the town that the Tourist Office in the Town Hall has available. Round the corner, just beyond the rue de l'Escaille at 20 rue de Bruxelles is the site of the Hotel de l'Escaille. In 1815, this was also a field hospital. This modern building now houses the Centre Public d'Aide Sociale, but it is not the original building.

Going out of the centre of Wavre in the direction of Louvain to the edge of town, there is a cemetery containing the memorial monument to the three Debève brothers, all Waterloo veterans.

Going in the opposite direction, towards Limal, one comes to the Bierges Mill. It is situated on the Dyle, upriver of Wavre. Close by is a memorial to General Gérard, who died in the fighting south-west of the mill.

One kilometre north of Wavre on the N4, the chaussée de Bruxelles, is a right turn when coming from the centre of Wavre, the chaussée Château de la Bawette. Up this steep hill is the Château of la Bawette that housed Thielemann's headquarters on 18/19 June. It is now the site of a golf club and visitors are asked to respect this.

Farm of la Bourse at Limal. The last artillery duel of the Battle of Wavre took place around here on 19 June 1815. (Inset) Memorial to General Gérard. This is close to the mill at Bierges, on the main road.

At some stage, it is worth taking a detour to Limal, 4km south-east of Wavre on the N37. One kilometre north of Limal on the rue J. Mathieu is the farm of La Bourse, the site of the final artillery duel at 3.30am on 19 June. Grouchy probably spent that night here.

Wavre to Plancenoit

Along this section of the campaign, there is little to show that there were any troop movements here. However, by following the route taken by the Prussians through the villages of Bierges and Rixensart to Chapelle-St-Lambert, one gets a good impression of the terrain they crossed. The roads they took were not paved at this time and the heavy rain of the previous day hindered movement, particularly by wheeled transport. The route was crossed by numerous ridges and by walking the route, one can gain an impression of the difficulties the Prussians faced.

Plancenoit

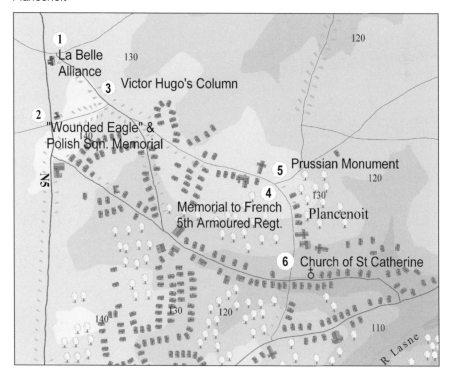

It is worth taking a look round when at Chapelle-St-Robert and Chapelle-St-Lambert, as one gains an impression of what the Prussians could perceive of what was facing them on the remainder of their march to Plancenoit. This road leads past the Ferme de la Kelle, which overlooks what was in 1815 the muddy defile down which the Prussians struggled with their runaway cannon towards Lasne.

On the far side of Lasne from the Ferme de la Kelle and about 4km north-east of Plancenoit stands the monument to Count Schwerin, the first Prussian officer killed in the Battle of Waterloo, who died in a skirmish with the troopers of Domon and Subervie. It consists of a column on a square pedestal surrounded by a hawthorn hedge. The inscription on the pedestal reads, 'Wilhelm, Count Schwerin, Royal Prussian Colonel and Knight, fell in the victory on 18 June 1815 in foreign lands for his country.'

Going down the Brussels to Charleroi highway from the Lion Mound, one comes to the road leading to Plancenoit. About 100 metres north of this junction is a memorial to the French 6th Foot Artillery that reads: 'From la Belle Alliance to Papelotte on 18 June 1815 units of Colonel Hulot's 6th Foot Artillery Regiment supported the attacks of the I French Corps with their effective fire.' On the corner of this road stands the former inn of la Belle Alliance, in another one of its reincarnations. On the wall on the highway side is a plaque in memory of the French Medical Corps 'that attended to wounded with devotion on 18 June 1815.'

Moving on from here towards the village of Plancenoit, one passes the site where some say Napoleon had his observation

Schwerin Memorial. On the edge of the site of the Bois de Paris, this column marks the place where the first fatal wounding of a Prussian officer occurred.

post. Continuing down this road, one passes a memorial to the French 5th Armoured Regiment (cuirassiers) that reads, 'On 18 June 1815, the 5th armoured regiment of Milhaud's Cavalry Corps departed from here to charge the squares of British infantry.'

Just down the road from here is the Prussian memorial, built by the famous architect Schinkel and put up in 1819. Damaged by marauding French soldiers in 1832, it was quickly repaired and railings placed around it to protect it. The inscription reads, 'To the dead heroes. The grateful King and Fatherland. May they rest in peace. La Belle Alliance, 18 June 1815.'

From here, one is drawn towards the church of St Catherine, passing the farm opposite the chapel of St Antoine that stood here in 1815. The current church of St Catherine is not the original, but was built in 1856. There are several memorials in and around this church. On the wall to the right of the entrance is a bronze plaque to the Young Guard and inside, on the left, near the altar, is a plaque to Lt Tattet. That to the Young Guard reads, 'In this village of Plancenoit the Young Guard of the Emperor Napoleon distinguished itself

Prussian Memorial at Plancenoit. Undergrowth hides this memorial.

on 18 June 1815. Commanded by Général Count Duhesme, who was mortally wounded.' That to Tattet reads, 'In memory of Jques Cles Adre Tattet, lieutenant of artillery of the Old Guard, member of the Legion of Honour, killed at the start of the battle of 18 June 1815 at the age of 22.'

The two other memorials at the church are that to Lt Louis and the French 8th Artillery Regiment. That to Louis is on the left wall of the church and reads, 'To Lieutenant M. Louis, 3rd Tirailleurs of the Guard, born in Jodoigne on 3.4.1787, died in Plancenoit 18.6.1815.' That to the 8th Artillery reads, 'From here on 18 June 1815, the 1st and 2nd Companies of

Plaque to the Young Guard. This is next to the entrance to the church.

Plaque to Lt. Louis of the Imperial Guard in Plancenoit.

Plaque to the French artillery in Plancenoit.

Memorial to the French 5th Line in Plancenoit.

the 8th Foot Artillery Regiment of Colonel Caron gave effective fire in support of the French VI Corps.'

A short walk from the church is a memorial to the French 5th Infantry Regiment that reads, 'From here on 18 June 1815, the 5th Line Infantry Regiment under Colonel Roussille of Simmer's Division heroically opposed the Prussian Corps of General von Bülow.'

There are still a number of original houses from the time with cellars where hand-to-hand fighting occurred. The farm on the hill above church was there in 1815 and the vicarage dates from 1789. It is worth wandering around the village to get an impression of what it must have been like in 1815.

Namur

Being 60km south-east of Brussels, Namur is a little out of the way, but well worth a visit. The tourist office near the train station in the centre of town has free maps available.

A plaque to the battle can be seen in the place d'Omalius, close to the railway station, at its western end at the beginning of the avenue des

Plaque in Namur commemorating Grouchy's rearguard action against the Prussians.

Memorial to Zastrow in the Belgrade Cemetery in Namur.

Plaque on the base of the Zastrow Memorial.

Combattants. This is where the Brussels Gate stood in 1815. The plaque reads, 'On 20 June 1815, this gate bore witness to the fighting of Marshal Grouchy's rearguard with the Prussian army'.

Going further up this road north-west along the chaussée de Waterloo in the direction of Gembloux, one comes to the cemetery of Belgrade, in the district of Saint-Servais, on the left of this road. Here, there is a monument to the Prussian Colonel von Zastrow, who was killed on 20 June in the fighting with Grouchy's men. It stands just to the left of the main entrance and was placed there by members of his regiment, the Colberg Infantry Regiment. The original engraving has deteriorated, but has been supplemented with a plaque. It reads 'The officer corps of the Regiment in memory of its brave leader'.

A monument to the French soldiers killed in the same incident is said to have been placed there as well, but does not appear to be there any longer.

The route to Paris

There is little to show of the events after Waterloo, except perhaps at Maubert-Fontaine, in France, 29km from Charleroi on the N39. There is a bakery here in what was the Hotel de Grand Turc, where Napoleon spent the evening of 19 June.

The fortresses

While there is little to see that denotes the events of 1815, many of the fortifications still exist and the towns they surround or are in are so charming that it is well worth making this tour for that reason alone. While not so much a battlefield trip, this tour is certainly of historical and architectural merit. These fortified places include:

Valenciennes 36km west of Mons. Sadly, there appears nothing of historical relevance to visit here.

Cambrai 29km south-west of Valenciennes. Both the citadel and some of the fortifications still survive.

Condé-sur-l'Escaut 11km north of Valenciennes. Some fortifications can still be seen.

Le Quesnoy 25km south-east of Valenciennes. Some of the fortifications are still in existence.

Landrecies 9km south of le Quesnoy. Inside the church on the right is a memorial to Henry Clarke, Duke of Feltre, who was Louis XVIII's minister of war during his exile in Ghent in the Hundred Days.

Maubeuge 21km south of Mons. Part of the fortifications still survives. On the former Gate of France is a plaque commemorating the defence of the town in 1814.

Avesnes-sur-Helpe 18km south of Maubeuge. As well as the Vauban fortifications, there is also a plaque to Napoleon on the wall of the rectory of the church of St Nicholas in the town centre. It commemorates Napoleon's stay there on the night of 13/14 June 1815 and reads, '13 June 1815. Napoleon I stayed in this old house, residence of the king's lieutenant, later the seat of the sub-prefecture, and issued his last general order before Waterloo here. – The Prince Imperial stayed here from 30 August to 2 September 1870 before going into exile.'

Napoleon's headquarters in Avesnes.

Plaque denoting Napoleon's residence in Avesnes.

Beaumont 30km north-east of Avesnes. As well as surviving fortifications, there is also the château of the Prince of Caraman-Chimay in the main town square where Napoleon stayed on the night of 14/15 June.

Philippeville 80km south of Brussels. Here, in the place de la Maison-du-Peuple stands the former Hôtel du Lion d'Or, where Napoleon rested for a few hours on 19 June. None of the fortifications assaulted by Prussians on 21 June still exist, but along the boulevard des Fortifications, near the ambulance station on the boulevard de l'Enseignment, is the old powder magazine, with a plaque. It is now a church, a case of a sword having being turned into a ploughshare.

Plaque on the former powder magazine in Philippeville.

Former Hôtel du Lion d'Or in Philippeville where Napoleon rested for a while on 19 June 1815.

Mariembourg 12km south of Philippeville. The Prussians demolished the fortifications in 1815 and there appears nothing of historical relevance to visit here.

Rocroi 34km south of Philippeville. Some of the fortifications here still exist.

Givet-Charlemont 22km east of Philippeville. Part of the fortifications here still exist, including the fortress of Charlemont.

Mézières-Charleville 53km south of Givet. Some of the fortifications here still exist.

Namur 60km south-east of Brussels. There is a museum in the citadel, as well as the memorials mentioned above.

Dinant 28km south of Namur. There is a military museum in the citadel, which stands on a rock 100 metres above the town.

Montmédy 62km south-east of Mézières. The citadel still exists.

Longwy 65km north-east of Metz. The citadel still exists.

While the fortress war of 1815 can be regarded as a footnote to the major events of the campaign, there is certainly much here for those interested in fortifications.

Orders of battle

Order of Battle, 18/20 June 1815

Army of the North (French)

Plancenoit   Napoleon Bonaparte

Imperial Guard   Marshal Mortier (absent)
Old Guard
1st Division   Count Roguet   (7)
2nd Division   Count Michel   (8)
Young Guard   Duhesme (?)
1st Brigade   Chartran   (4)
2nd Brigade   Guye   (4)
Light Cavalry   Count Lefebvre-Desnoëttes   (13) (At Quatre Bras)
Reserve Cavalry   Baron Guyot   (13)
Artillery   (96)

6th Corps   Count Lobau
19th Division   Baron Zimmer
  Brigade   Baron de Bellair   (5)
  Brigade   Jamin   (4)
  Artillery   (8)
20th Division   Jeannin
  Brigade   Bony   (4)
  Brigade   Tromelin   (3)
  Artillery   (8)
Artillery   (16?)

Wavre   Count Grouchy

3rd Corps   Count Vandamme
8th Division   Baron Lefol
  Brigade   Billard   (6)
  Brigade   Baron Corsin   (5)
  Artillery   (8)
10th Division   Baron Habert
  Brigade   Baron Gengoult   (6)
  Brigade   Duperyoux   (6)
  Artillery   (8)

11th Division   Baron Berthezène
  Brigade   Baron Dufour   (4)
  Brigade   Baron Lagarde   (4)
  Artillery   (8)
Artillery   (8)

4th Corps	Count Gérard	
12th Division	Baron Pêcheux	
Brigade	Rome	(6)
Brigade	Schaeffer	(4)
Artillery		(8)
13th Division	Baron Vichery	
Brigade	Le Capitaine	(4)
Brigade	Desprez	(4)
Artillery		(8)
14th Division	Hulot	
Brigade	Hulst	(4)
Brigade	Toussaint	(4)
Artillery		(8)
7th Cavalry Division	Maurin	
Brigade	Vallin	(6)
Brigade	Berruyer	(8)
Artillery		(6)
Artillery		(8)
21st Division	Baron Teste	(From 6th Corps)
Brigade	Lafitte	(4)
Brigade	Penne	(3)
Artillery		(8)

1st Cavalry Corps	Count Pajol	
4th Cavalry Division	Soult	(12+6)
5th Cavalry Division	Subervie	(11+6) (Detached)

2nd Cavalry Corps	Count Exelmans	
9th Cavalry Division	Baron Strolz	(16+6)
10th Cavalry Division	Baron Chastel	(15+6)

Notes – The number in brackets indicates the number of battalions (infantry), squadrons (cavalry) or guns (artillery). The number after a '+' sign indicates the number of guns attached to a cavalry division.

Order of Battle 18 June 1815

Army of the Lower Rhine (Prussian)   Field Marshal General Prince Gebhardt Leberecht Blücher von Wahlstadt

At Waterloo / Plancenoit

I Army Corps	Zieten	
1st Brigade	Steinmetz	(9? + 4 + 8)
2nd Brigade	Pirch II	(9 + 4 + 7)
3rd Brigade	Jagow	(9? + 0 + 8)
4th Brigade	Henckel von Donnersmarck	(6 + 0 + 8)

Reserve Cavalry	Roeder	
1st Brigade	Treschkow II	(12 + 8)
2nd Brigade	Lützow	(12 + 8)
Reserve Artillery	Rentzell	(39)
II Army Corps	Pirch I	
5th Brigade	Tippelskirch	(9 + 2 + 8)
6th Brigade	Krafft	(9 + 2 + 8)
7th Brigade	Brause	(9 + 2 + 8)
8th Brigade	Bose	(9 + 2 + 7)
Reserve Cavalry	Wahlen-Jürgass	
1st Brigade	Thümen	(12 + 8)
2nd Brigade	Sohr	(8)
3rd Brigade	Schulenberg	(8)
Reserve Artillery	Lehmann	(40)
IV Army Corps	Bülow	
13th Brigade	Hake	(9 + 2 + 8)
14th Brigade	Ryssel	(9 + 2 + 8)
15th Brigade	Losthin	(9 + 2 + 8)
16th Brigade	Hiller	(9 + 2 + 8)
Reserve Cavalry	Prince William of Prussia	
1st Brigade	Count Schwerin	(12 + 8)
2nd Brigade	Watzdorff	(3 + 8)
3rd Brigade	Sydow	(20)
Reserve Artillery	Bardeleben	(40)

At Wavre

III Army Corps	Thielemann	
9th Brigade	Borcke	(9 + 2 + 8)
10th Brigade	Kemphen	(6 + 2 + 8)
11th Brigade	Luck	(6 + 2 + 0)
12th Brigade	Stülpnagel	(9 + 2 + 0)
Reserve Cavalry	Hobe	
1st Brigade	Marwitz	(7)
2nd Brigade	Lottum	(9 + 8)
Reserve Artillery	Grevenitz	(24)

Notes – Prussian brigades were the equivalent of divisions in other armies. The first figure in brackets is the number of infantry battalions or cavalry squadrons, the second the number of cavalry squadrons (attached to an infantry brigade) and the final figures the number of guns.

North German Federal Army Corps

Commanding General: General Count Kleist von Nollendorf (later Lt-General von Hake)
Commanding General, Hessian contingent: Lt-General Engelhardt

1st (Hessian) Brigade: Major-General Prince zu Solms-Braunfels

2nd Grenadier Battalion von Lassberg	(1)
Infantry Regiment Landgraf Karl	(2)
Infantry Regiment Prince Solms	(2)

2nd (Hessian) Brigade: Major-General von Müller

1st Grenadier Battalion von Haller	(1)
Infantry Regiment Kurfürst	(3)
Infantry Regiment Kurprinz	(2)
Jäger Battalion	(1)

(Hessian) Cavalry Brigade: Major-General von Warburg (Prussian)

Life Dragoon Regiment	(4)
Hussar Regiment	(4)

(Hessian) Artillery

6 Pounder Battery No. 1	(8)
6 Pounder Battery No. 2	(8)

3rd (Anhalt-Thuringian) Brigade: Colonel von Egloffstein (Weimar)

1st Provisional Infantry Regiment	(4)
2nd Provisional Infantry Regiment	(4)
3rd Provisional Infantry Regiment	(2/3)
Oldenburg Line Infantry Regiment	(2)

Recommended further reading

A popular subject like the Waterloo Campaign has attracted considerable attention, making it difficult to do more than highlight a few works that make good further reading. Some are modern, some are classics and they have been chosen to provide different perspectives to the Campaign.

Adkin, Mark *The Waterloo Companion*, London, 2001

Boulger, Demetrius C. *The Belgians at Waterloo*, London, 1901 and recently reprinted

Chalfont, Lord (ed), *Waterloo – Battle of Three Armies*, London, 1979

Dallas, Gregor *1815 – The Roads to Waterloo* London, 1996

Hofschröer, Peter *1815 – The Waterloo Campaign* 2 vols, London 1998-99

Hofschröer, Peter *Wellington's Smallest Victory* London, 2004

Houssaye, Henri *1815 – Waterloo* London, 1900 and various reprints

Siborne, Major-General Herbert Taylor *Waterloo Letters* London, 1891 and various reprints

Siborne, Capt. William *History of the Waterloo Campaign* 3rd ed., London, 1848 and various reprints

Speeckaert, Georges Patrick and Baecker, Isabelle *Relics and Memorials of the Battles of 1815 in Belgium* Lasne, 2000

Websites

Waterloo Tourist Office
www.waterloo-tourisme.be

Waterloo Visitors Centre
www.waterloo1815.be

Waterloo – The Three Commanders
http://www.bbc.co.uk/history/war/waterloo/three_commanders_01.shtml

Waterloo 1815 – The Belgian Contribution
http://www.geocities.com/waterloo1815be/index.html

If Napoleon Had Won the Battle of Waterloo
http://www.geocities.com/Athens/Forum/7227/ifnapwon.htm

IGN maps

The Belgian Institute Géographique Nationale (Nationaal Geografisch Institut) offers a series of scale maps. The ones of relevance to this tour include:

1:100,000

109 – Brussels
111 – Mons–Charleroi
112 – Namur–Huy
114 – Chimay–Dinant

1:50,000

40 – Wavre
45 – Mons
46 – Charleroi
47 – Namur
52 – Thuin
53 – Dinant
57 – Chimay
58 – Philippeville

1:10,000 and 1:25,000 or 1:20,000

40 – Wavre
45 – Mons
46 – Charleroi
47 – Namur
52 – Thuin
53 – Dinant
57 – Chimay
58 – Philippeville

Militair Toerisme – Tourisme Militaire Belgique - België

Further details can be found on: www.ign.be and www.ngi.be.

Index

Aisemont 18
Aisne (river) 82
Alsace 77
Anderlues 74, 75
Anglesey, Marquis of See Uxbridge, Earl of Anglo-Dutch-German Army – 1st Netherlands Division 87
Anglo-Dutch-German Army – King's German Legion (KGL) 29
Anglo-Dutch-German Army – Nassau Contingent 29, 44, 50, 51
Antwerp 27
Ardennes 98
Argenteuil 86
August, Prince 67 (biography), 80, 87, 93, 95, 98
Automne (river) 83
Avesnes (-sur-Helpe) (77), (78), 87, 121, (122), 123
Baraque 70
Baisy 29
Bas-Wavre 68, 69
Bavay 79
Bawette 13, 18, 112
Beaumont 75, 122
Belle Alliance 29, 30, 55
Bernhard of Saxe-Weimar, Duke 29, 44, 46, 50, 51
Bierges 34, 36, 68, 113
Bierges Mill (17), 18, 67, 70, 71
Blücher von Wahlstadt, Field Marshal General Prince 7, 10, 11, 14, 19, 20, 21 (biography), 27, 31, 41, 46, (56), 57, (58), (59), 61, 62, 66, 68, 74, 75, 76, 77, 80, 81, 82, 86, 87, 94, 95, 102, 106
Bonaparte, Napoleon See Napoleon
Bonne Villiers 63
Bonlez 23
Bonnichon, General 97
Boquet 75
Borcke, General von 68

Bose, General von 95
Bouchain 88
Bouillon 87, 96
Braine l'Alleud 29
Brussels 23, 27, 29, 64, 66, 67, 73, 110, 123, 124
Brye 11, 110
Bülow von Dennewitz, Lt-General Count 10, 13, 19, 20, 23, 24 (biography), 33, 34, 35, 36, 38, 39, 41, 42, 43, 44, 46, 48, 51, 61, 66, 74, 75, 77, 79, 81, 82, 83, 86
Burke, General Count 95, 96
Byng, General 28
Caillou (60), 62
Cambrai 81, 87, 121
Capelle 81
Cassaigne, General 92, 93
Catillon 87
Chantelet (farm) (30)
Chantelet (wood) 62
Chapelle-St-Lambert (33), 35, 36, 39, 42, 113, 114
Chapelle-St-Robert 114
Charlemont 94, 95, 96
Charleroi 62, 63, 74, 75, 121
Charleville (-Mézières) 87, 97, 98
Chartrand, General 54
Châtillon 86
Chaumont 23
Chiers 99
Chimay 79, 80
Choisy, Baron 96
Clarke, Henry 121
Colville, General 81
Compiègne 82, 83
Condé (-sur-l'Escaut) 87, 88, 90, 121
Constant Rebecque, Baron de 60
Corbais 20, 64
Corry-le-Grand 20, 23
Creil 82

Davoût, Marshal 81
D'Erlon, Count Drouet 30, 44, 79
Dinant 78, 79, 124
Dion-le-Mont 13, 20, 23, 32
Dixon, Colonel 89
Domon, General 30, 36, 44, 46, 114
Dörnberg; Major-General von 29
Douai 88
Duhesme, General 50, (54)
Durette, General 44
Dyle (river) 13, (17), 18, 20, 29, 33, 34, 66, 67, 69
Exelmans, General 20, 33
Fère 82, 87
Fichermont 35, 38, 46, 50, (51)
Fontaine-l'Evêque 74, 75
France, Army - Imperial Guard 7, (9), (22), 30, 38, 44, 49, 51, 53, 55, 57, 62, 75, 82, 83, 106, (116)
France, Army – Young Guard 43, 50, 51, 53, 54, 83, 106, 115, (116)
France, Army – Guard Cavalry (10), 30
Frederik, Prince 53 (biography), 87
Froidmont 36, 38, 48
Gembloux 10, 14, 15, 19, 64, 73, 75, 110
Genappe 20, 29, 30, 55, 57, 63
Gentinnes 20
Genval 48
Gérard, Count 64, 69 (biography), 70, 73, 75
Gerpinnes 80
Gilocourt 82, 83
Girard, General 9
Givet (-Charlemont) 79, 87, 93, 94, 95, 96, 124
Glabais 30
Gonesse 83, 86
Goumont See: Hougoumont
Gneisenau, Lt-General Count von 7, 10, 15, 20, 23, 27, 28 (biography), 63, 74, 76
Grant, Major-General 29
Grouchy, Count 9, 14, 15, 18, 36, 41, 64, 65 (biography), 66, 67, 70, 72, 73, 74,

75, 78, 79, 80, 81, 82, 83, 86, 101, 110
Guise 81
Habert, General 68, 69
Hake, Lt-General von 23, 33, 42, 97, 98, 99, 109
Hardinge, Lt-Col Sir Henry 10, (11)
Haye Sainte 29, 43, 51
Hesse-Homburg, Lt General Prince 99
Hiller, General von 23, 33, 36, 42, 46, 48, 49, 53, 55
Hirson 80, 81
Hougoumont 29, 30, 43
Houille (river) 95
Hulot, Colonel 70, 114
Issy 87
Jackson, Lt Basil 59
Jacquinot, General 30, 44
Jagow, General von 87
Jeanin, General 36
Jérôme 75
Kelle (farm) 39, (40)
Kellermann, General 9, 30
Kleist von Nollendorf, General 79, 109
Krafft, Major-General von 90, 95
Landrecies 79, 87, 90, 91, 93, 121
Laon 79, 80, 81, 82, 87
Laplanche, General 97
Lasne 39, 42, 46
Lasne brook 38, 41, 44, 49
Laurent, General 98
Lauzelle 11
Lefebvre-Desnoëttes, General 83
Lehmann, Colonel 79
Lemoine, General 97, 98
Liège 14, 66, 94
Ligny 9, 10, 27
Lille 88
Limal 34, (112), 113
Limelette 67
Lobau, Count 9, 30, 31 (biography), 36, 44, 47, 48, 49, 53, 57, 68, 75
Longwy 87, 98, 99, 124
Lorraine 80

Losthin, General von 23, 33, 34, 42, 46, 47, 49
Louis XVIII 80, 81, 87, 88, 90, 91, 95, 98, 99, 121
Lowe, Sir Hudson 59
Luck, Colonel von 68, 69
Luxembourg 87, 94, 98
Maison du Roi 29, 59, 60
Maransart 37
Mariembourg 79, 80, 87, 124
Marle 81
Maubert-Fontaine 81
Maubeuge 75, 79, 87, 88, 89, 90, 93, 121
Mazy 64
Médy 98, 99
Mellery 11, 19, 20, 110
Merlen, Major-General van 29
Meuse (river) 77, 81, 94, 96, 97
Metz 99, 100, 124
Mézières (-Charleville) 81, 97, 124
Milhaud, General 9, 115
Mohon 98
Mons 74, 121
Montmédy 98, 99, 124
Mont St Guibert 15, 38
Mont St Jean 29, 30
Morand, General 53
Moselle (river) 81
Müffling, Major-General von 48, 51, 59
Nanteuil 83
Namur 10, 11, 14, 15, 55, 64, 67, 75, 77, 78, 110, 118, 124
Napoleon 7, 8, 12 (biography), 14, 15, 18, 19, (22), 29, 30, 31, 35, 36, 37, 38, 39, 41, 42, 44, 46, 48, 49, 50, 51, 53, 54, 55, (56), 57, 64, 66, 67, 73, 74, 75, 76, 80, 88, 94, 105
Ney, Marshal Michel 9, 27, 44, 51, (52), 101
Nivelles 73, 74
North German Federal Army Corps 78, 79, 80, 87, 93, 96, 97, 98, 108
Ohain 37, 39, 48
Oise (river) 81, 82
Orange, Prince of 60

Ouse (river) 90
Pajol, General 64, 72, 75
Papelotte 29, 43, (45)
Paris 8
Paris, Convention of 87
Paris Wood 34, 36, 38, 39, 42, 44
Pelet, General 53, 54
Péronne 87
Perwez 15
Philippeville 75, 76, 79, 80, 87, 91, (92), 93, 95, (123), 124
Pirch I, Major-General von 10, 11, 13, 19, 20, 34 (biography), 36, 55, 89
Pirch II, Major-General von 83
Plaige, Colonel 90, 91
Plancenoit 7, 30, 32, 33, 34, 39, (43), (44), 46, 47, 48, (49), 51, 53, 54, 55, 57, 59, 60, 61, 62, 114, (115)
Pont du Christ (Wavre) (15), 68, 110
Ponsonby, General 29
Prix 98
Projean, General 93
Prussia Army – I Army Corps 68
Prussia Army – II Army Corps 80, 87, 89
Prussia Army – IV Army Corps 67, 90, 97
Prussia Army – VI Army Corps 99
Quatre Bras 9, 14, 20, 27, 28, 101
Quesnoy 79, 87, 88, 121
Reiche, General von 48, 51
Reille, Count 9, 30, 64, 79, 83
Rethel 81, 82
Rheims 82
Rhineland 11, 94
Rixensart 113
Rixensart Wood 71
Rocroi 80, 81, 87, 95, 124
Roeder, General von 62, 63
Rossomme 59, 60
Roy, General 88
Ryssel, General von 23, 33, 36, 42, 50
St-Agatha-Rode 75
St Anne 13
St Denis 86

St Germain 86
St Lambert 34, 36, 38, 39, 42
St Laurent 98
St Quentin 82
Sambre (river) 73, 74, 75, 82, 87, 88, 89, 90
Sart-à-Walhain 15
Schwerin, Count 42, (114)
Sedan 78, 87, 96, 97
Seine (river) 86, 90
Senlis 82
Serre (river) 82
Siborne, Capt. William 110
Simmer, General 36, 49
Smohain 29, 50
Soissons 80, 81, 82, 83, 87
Sombreffe 19
Somerset, General 29
Somme (river) 83
Soult, Marshal 70
Souvret 75
Stains 83
Steinmetz, Major-General von 48
Subervie, General 30, 36, 114
Temploux 64
Teste, General 14
Thielemann, Lt-General von 8, 10, 13, 14, 18, 19, 20, 23, 47 (biography), 67, 68, 70, 72, 73, 74, 75, 82, 86, 113
Thionville 99
Thuin 80
Tienen 64
Tilly 11, 110
Tourinnes 15, 20
Tour-Maubourg, Count de la 89
Tout Vent 23
Uxbridge, Earl of 29
Valenciennes 79, 87, 88, 121

Valentini 39
Vandamme, Count d'Unsebourg 9, 14, 64, 70, 71 (biography), 81, 82, 83, 86, 87
Vandeleur, General 29
Vauban 88, 90, 93, 94
Vendée 77
Vermand 82
Versailles 86
Vervins 79, 81
Vichery, General 80, 81
Virère Wood 49
Vieux Sart 33
Villecourt 83
Villecourt-Cotterêts 83
Vivian, Sir Richard Hussey 8, 29, 48
Walcourt 80
Walhain (-St-Paul) 20, (42), (43), 110
Warcq 98
Waterloo 8, 18, 23, 27, 28, 29, 34, 36, 40, 59, 64, 66, 67, 68, 74, 75, 121
Wavre 7, 8, 10, 11, 13, 14, 15, 17, 18, 19, 23, 27, 33, 64, 67, 68, 69, 70, 72, 75, 110, 113
Wellington, Duke of 7, 9, 11, 14, 16 (biography), 20, 23, 27, 28, 31, 34, 38, 39, 41, 42, 44, 46, 48, 49, 50, 51, 53, 54, 55, (56), 57, (58), (59), 60, 61, 64, 66, 71, 80, 81, 82, 86, 87, 88, 95, 101
Zastrow, Colonel von (119), (120)
Zieten, Lt-General Count von 7, 10, 11, 13, 20, 23, 36, 37 (biography), 48, 50, 51, 62, 63, 72, 74, 75, 77, 78, 79, 81, 82, 83, 86

NB – Numbers in brackets indicate an illustration.